# OWN YOUR INDUSTRY

## DOUGLAS KRUGER

PORTFOLIO
PENGUIN

First published by Penguin Books (South Africa) (Pty) Ltd, 2014
A Penguin Random House company
Registered Offices: Block D, Rosebank Office Park, 181 Jan Smuts Avenue, Parktown North, Johannesburg 2193, South Africa
www.penguinbooks.co.za
Copyright © Douglas Kruger 2014
All rights reserved
The moral right of the author has been asserted
ISBN 978-0-14-353860-8
eISBN 978-0-14-353121-0
Text design and typesetting by Hybrid Illustration & Design
Cover design by publicide
Printed and bound by CTP Printers, Cape Town
Except in the United States of America, this book is sold subject to the condition that it shall not, by way of trade or otherwise, be lent, resold, hired out or otherwise circulated without the publisher's prior consent in any form of binding other than that in which it is published and without a similar condition including this condition being imposed on the subsequent purchaser.

For my wife, Vanessa, for her expertise in matters of the heart
and of patience ... and for her astonishing ability to make the best
"death-by-potatoes" the world has ever seen!

"Talent is cheaper than table salt. What separates the talented individual from the successful one is a lot of hard work." – Stephen King

Stephen King, arguably the world's bestselling living author, reads a novel every three days, amounting to 119 unique instances of study of his craft per annum. Makes you think …

"If you build it, they will come …" – *Field of Dreams*

# CONTENTS

Foreword by Stuart Loxton — viii

Foreword by Jim Key — ix

Acknowledgments — xi

Premise — 1

The Pie Man and the Guru — 2

The expert phenomenon — 4

Why bother? — 6

Does your sales team need more training? Or does your thought leadership need work? — 8

"Yikes! I can't be an expert! Why, I'm no more than a terrified marshmallow …!" — 11

Which philosophy? — 16

What it will take to design "you" — 17

The culture of living as an expert — 21

## 50 ways to Position yourself as an expert — 25

1. Understand the science of talent — 26
2. Determine your values — 31
3. Outwork the competition — 33
4. Start asking the "Constant Question" — 36
5. Devour knowledge — 38
6. Find a niche — 40
7. Be a producer — 43
8. Be a face and a voice — 46
9. Be credible by association — 48
10. Dress the part — 50
11. Act the part — 52
12. Learn the names — 54
13. Develop a title — 56
14. Use simple positioning — 58
15. Develop a story of struggle — 60
16. Find a way to be the most or the greatest — 62
17. Develop a free educational guide — 64
18. Hoard and publicise praise — 66
19. Speak the language of results — 68
20. Gather paying clients — 71
21. Be declarative and state what you are an expert in — 73
22. Develop products — 75
23. Offer your expertise to the media — 80
24. Use social media — 85
25. Acquire third party endorsements — 89
26. Develop partnerships and sponsorships — 91
27. Add your unique signature to your work — 93
28. Develop a unique framework philosophy — 95
29. Manage popularity by design — 98
30. Gain extraordinary visibility — 102
31. Unify the tone of your branding and communications — 104
32. Control important positioning scenarios — 106
33. Do what you say you will do — 109
34. Be the one who responds — 111
35. Make the other look good — 113
36. Be politically astute — 115
37. Price yourself at the right level — 117

38. Have your customers sell to you                              121
39. Give guarantees                                              123
40. Start with a tool box                                        126
41. Determine some passion points                                129
42. Find an opportunity to give value                            132
43. Use the Thought-Leadership formula                           135
44. Speak with strength                                          137
45. Use the incredible power of metaphors                        141
46. Stories are your very best friends                           143
47. Frame issues and create urgency                              145
48. Constantly manufacture messages                              147
49. Get much, much more mileage out of an idea                   149
50. Experts always leave a trail of breadcrumbs                  152

Practical mechanics                                              154

Bonus section: 15 Ways to win contests                           157

Some final thoughts                                              162

References                                                       170

# FOREWORD BY STUART LOXTON

Careers evolve over time. Not just the careers of individuals, but the very *nature* of careers. There was a time when it was enough to be solidly competent at your craft. The shoemaker made his shoes, he sold them, and the shoes, in turn, were expected to carry out their purpose adequately. Nothing more. People purchased the shoes, and thought no more about them than to evaluate whether or not they worked.

And indeed, you can still get by that way today. In the story of your life, no one is forcing you to do any more than to make an adequate shoe. And if you do, you can sell it for an adequate fee. It will fund an adequate life.

I've worked with many such people in many different corporate companies. Interestingly, I don't select them for my teams, and I don't call on them for important projects.

Becoming an expert, however, changes the way you work. It changes the way people value your work and it changes the public perception of the story of your life, making it more noteworthy. These are the people I value, the ones I seek out, and this is the kind of person I always aspire to be in my own working life.

With that in mind, why *wouldn't* you choose to be an expert? Why wouldn't you choose to be the *Armani* of shoemakers?

This is your life. Make the choice. Begin with the decision to be – as Douglas puts it – *the best* in your field. Then dive into these pages and discover the many practical ways to realise that ambition.

Douglas's book is like a map for career growth. It is every bit as well suited to the private entrepreneur as it is to the ambitious employee. Combining principles of PR and personal excellence, *Own Your Industry* is as relevant to the CEO as it is to his or her sales team. In fact, it is *particularly* relevant to sales teams. Read it, and find out why ...

Careers evolve over time. This has always been the case, and it will continue to be going forward. So, do you have it in you to make the tough choice? Or will you leave this world having been ... *adequate*?

Go out and make excellent shoes!

**Stuart Loxton**
**Executive Director, Fairbairn Capital of Old Mutual**

# FOREWORD BY JIM KEY

In today's world, the value of having an expert is undeniable. Knowing that someone whose experience you can benefit from stands ready to assist you can be reassuring. Being that someone – being recognised as the indisputable go-to person on a particular topic – brings with it deserved prestige, respect and professional advancement.

But how do you achieve the recognition of being an expert in your chosen field?

When I met Douglas Kruger in August 2004 at the Toastmasters International Convention, it was clear to me that he knew something about accomplishing things. I was the reigning World Champion of Public Speaking at the time, and Douglas was vying to become my successor.

I worked with Douglas briefly in his preparation for the contest and I found him to be very impressive. The rate at which he assimilated input and advice and weighed it against how it might serve his purpose, all the while under a significant time deadline was impressive to say the least. It was obvious he was a person who made things happen.

That Douglas's accomplishments are impressive is an understatement. I don't know anyone else who's been a public speaking champion for an entire nation five separate times. In addition, his career as a broadcaster, author, speaker and trainer, who has presented in nations around the world, clearly shows Douglas is a master communicator: an expert in his field.

Irish playwright George Bernard Shaw is quoted as saying:

> The people who get on in this world are the people who get up and look for the circumstances they want, and, if they can't find them, make them.

It is not enough simply to possess some knowledge, some ability, or some special quality. To get ahead you must have the ability or create the circumstances to raise your visibility, to publicise that you have that knowledge, ability or quality, in order to benefit from it.

Douglas is a person who has done exactly that. He has successfully positioned himself as an expert. But that's only part of the story. Not content to simply be an expert, Douglas has penned this book to share the tips and techniques, the secrets and the strategies that will enable you to do the same.

As you read this, you'll identify practical things you can do to become better recognised in your field. As you begin to do those things, your name will surface as the expert of choice for your future clients and your business will prosper.

Just be sure to send Douglas a thank you note when they do!

**Jim Key**
**2003 Public Speaking World Champion**

## ACKNOWLEDGEMENTS

I've always had the most incredible experiences with experts. Toastmasters World Champions like David Brooks, Jim Key, Randy Harvey and other giants have been nothing but generous with their time and expertise, doling out nuggets of gold for free and extending their friendship without reservation.

I find this to be true of most great men and women.

I offer my heartfelt thanks to these legends, not only for the specific information they so willingly impart, not merely for the light they bring into the world, but also for being solidly decent, dependable, genuinely caring human beings.

I'll never forget the day when, after returning from a failed World Championships speaking bid to the loneliness of a hotel room, David Brooks, a World Champion himself, found my number, called me up and took me out to dinner. Just to chat. Just to see how I was doing. These are good people, and the world is richer for their like.

I'd like to thank my editors, Pascale Barrow and Madeleine Kruger, for bringing their expert eyes to these pages.

And finally, my thanks and praise to the Alpha and Omega, the Light and the Life, the One Great Expert. I can write the odd book, give the odd speech. But You made the stars in the night sky. *Love* Your work!

# PREMISE

- Premium positioning is a choice, just as wealth is a choice, and no one else can make the choice for you.
- The barrier to entry for thought leadership exists only in your mind. If you have the courage to try, chances are that you can become an industry thought leader.
- It is almost impossible to get rich without working hard. However, it is entirely possible to work hard and never get rich. Perceived expertise determines the difference in the value of your work.

These are the pillar observations upon which expert positioning is built. Welcome to a small shift in perceptions that can equate to a quantum shift in your industry positioning. Let's change your place in the food chain.

# THE PIE MAN AND THE GURU

**THE PIE MAN WENT TO MARKET. THE GURU MADE THE MARKET COME TO HIM.**

Picture them. A large, broiling crowd gathered at the scene of a spectacle. They are noisy, multitudinous and made up of as many colours, races, faces and tongues as the nations have created. They are your target market. And wherever they gather, you will find him: The Pie Man.

Most business owners and entrepreneurs today act like the long-suffering Pie Man of old. Watch him as he moves about. You can see him fussing at the outskirts, tapping each person on the shoulder and asking whether they would like a pie. Most say no. Sometimes, someone says yes, and then the Pie Man makes a sale. He hands over his pie. In return, he receives a coin. This represents the totality of his business model.

It's a lot of work to sell a single pie and the Pie Man must keep up his incessant to and fro in order to sell the next one, and then the next, if he hopes to survive.

You do not want to be the Pie Man in your industry. So what is the alternative?

Cast your eyes over the heads of the crowd and observe who they have come to see. There in the distance, elevated on the hillside, is the Guru. He is the one that the crowd have assembled to see. They have gathered in the hope of hearing him speak. They have come to him. *That's* who you want to be.

Tapping shoulders and selling pies is tedious, costly and time-consuming. It's termed cold-calling, and it is the most soul-grinding of the various business models. It represents the highest maintenance sales approach and the least certain thing in the long run.

Business – and life generally – becomes a different proposition when *they* start coming to *you*. When you become noted as the foremost name in your industry, as a guru, an *expert*, a wonderful thing starts to happen. Instead of fussing and fighting for every incidental customer, you suddenly discover that the crowds begin flocking to you. That's how you want to go about it. Be the guru.

# THE EXPERT PHENOMENON

Over time, their voices become familiar. You come to like them, to listen to them and to believe them. When we discuss an industry, their faces float to mind. Without having to think about it, we tag their names to the end of the sentence "You know who you should talk to about that …?"

These are the gurus, the thought leaders, the icons. When the big names are in need of guidance, when the media requires insights, and when high-paying customers are ready to spend, they are the go-to people.

But experts are never experts by accident. They are the men and women who are highly publicised in their industry. They have worked hard for their place in our perceptions. And while it's true that they have built up a considerable body of knowledge, there is also a significant public relations element to their stature. They are who they are because they have crafted that reputation over time, and they have done so on purpose.

The good news is that their techniques *can* be emulated. As you build your business and brand, in your presentations, pitches and writing, in your networking and socialising, it is entirely possible to position yourself as an industry expert on purpose, to become iconic by design.

This book provides you with 50 specific techniques for achieving the goal of positioning yourself as an expert. Use any of the ways individually or use a number of them in conjunction to enhance how others perceive you.

As you grow in mastery, use what you learn to benefit others and not to harm. Positioning yourself as an expert will increase your wealth, influence and capacity. But understand that doing so will make you a leader, and that has consequences for everyone. Be a *good* leader.

Use the resulting influence for the good of those whom you lead and influence. After all, if you are perceived to be at the top of the pile, it means that you're standing on the shoulders of others. If you're at the forefront of your field, it means that others are following you. Lead them to prosperity and to success and they will continue to support you over time. Exploit them and they will abandon you. Guide them wisely and you will be called great.

Good luck as you embark on your voyage to guru-dom!

# WHY BOTHER?

Expert positioning is hard work. So why would you go to the extra trouble above and beyond the work you are already doing in your career?

There are three benefits to positioning yourself as an industry expert:

**1. THE BUSINESS STARTS COMING TO YOU**

When you are unknown, you have to cold-call to generate business. When you are iconic, the business comes to you. People desire association with your name or brand. This switch in your business dynamic is a singularly satisfying moment in the life of an entrepreneur. It is also in no small part lucrative.

I spent years building up a reputation as a speaker, struggling with the frustration of being unknown and having to tap people on the shoulder to sell my proverbial pies. But over time, my writing and marketing activities caught up with me. The day I received two calls from senior managers at large multinational companies, within the same half hour – both asking for training for their senior staff – was the day that I realised my positioning was working.

I didn't make sales calls to either of these organisations. I had had no prior contact with them. In both cases, I was simply recommended by somebody else. When I took the calls, both people remarked, "Someone told me that you are the person to talk to."

I would like that to start happening for you.

## 2. YOU CAN ADD AN EXTRA ZERO TO YOUR INCOME

There are many ways of earning an income. You can labour all day and earn minimum wage. Or you can be recognised as a leading authority and earn exponentially more for shorter periods of input.

In this latter model, hours of work no longer determine your remuneration. Instead, the very *status* of your work has been elevated, and people pay you in accordance with that perception. Perceived expertise is worth more money.

Here's a practical example: a mid-level consultant works for a large organisation, concludes his business and hands in an invoice for Rx. But Richard Branson drops by to speak on business principles, and the same organisation adds three extra zeroes to his cheque. Is it because Branson worked harder? No, it is because of the very equity of his name. Being Richard Branson is worth a lot of money.

Of course, that's not to say becoming an expert can *replace* hard work. It is extremely hard work to get there in the first place. But the rewards then become relative to your perceived status.

## 3. IT IS DEEPLY FULFILLING

Finally, being an expert provides a sense of career and personal satisfaction that is unparalleled. There is nothing quite so fulfilling as rising above the status of a small cog in a big machine, and being able to comment upon, advise and solve issues that cause a great deal of anxiety for others.

Being a "solutions" person is a rewarding station. You'll enjoy a blend of the kind of "groupies and glory" vibe that rock stars thrive upon – although experts generally enjoy a *manageable* degree of celebrity – right alongside the altruistic glow experienced by the charitable of heart. You'll be looked up to, respected and admired. But best of all, you'll be genuinely helping others and getting paid well for it.

What could be more rewarding?

Of course, no one is forcing you to elevate your positioning. If you really want to, you *can* spend the rest of your days as the industry pie man ...

## DOES YOUR SALES TEAM NEED MORE TRAINING? OR DOES YOUR THOUGHT LEADERSHIP NEED WORK?

---

Most of these pages deal with the idea of individuals as experts. But there is no doubt that companies and brands can be seen as experts too. There is also no doubt that they can do so on purpose, or that they *should*. Because sometimes, when sales are down, it's not about the sales …

**LET YOUR FINGERS DO THE WALKING**

In 2010, I was asked to present at the annual "sales kick-off" for a national gathering of the *Yellow Pages*. They were still feeling the pinch of the recession and loyal clients were hesitant to advertise as liberally as before. Oh sure, they had the funds. But they also had *fear*. They were hesitant to spend, more conscious of outgoing cash and more determined than ever to see clear value for their money.

The *Yellow Pages* sales team were well trained in sales techniques. They were accustomed to moving big numbers. But the problem persisted.

In my keynote presentation, "How to Sell in Tough Times", I pointed out:

If your clients have the money to spend …
And they need what you're offering …
But they're still not buying what you're offering …
Even though it would be good for them to do so …
Then the problem lies in a single word:
Perceptions!

I unpacked the idea that sometimes, when sales are down, it's not about the sales team. They're working every bit as hard as before, sometimes even harder. The problem lies with *how your client views the world.* Or again: their perceptions.

The *Yellow Pages* faced a number of perception issues:

1. An economy full of hesitant buyers.
2. The widespread notion that the *Yellow Pages* was nothing but an obsolete, dusty old book no one used any more, and who uses paper these days anyway? (Which wasn't true because they had a massive online presence.)
3. The fact that there were so many new ways to advertise, that the whole business of advertising is now just plain confusing.

Of course, if you're not ruled by the fear of the moment, and you can keep your head about you in times of crisis, you'll see opportunities everywhere. This particular crisis represented a *massive* opportunity for the *Yellow Pages.* It was an opportunity to address perceptions, and position themselves as thought leaders.

How? Here's how:

1. If the economy is full of hesitant buyers, they needed to tell people that the recession was over (using valid stats and story-examples). And they needed to champion the message: "Now is the time to advertise again!" They needed to be persuasive on this point because it's true (firstly) and because their business depended upon it.
2. If people saw the *Yellow Pages* as old, their job was to address that perception and convince them that they're using the latest cutting-edge approaches to online advertising (which they were). If nobody even knows you are doing this, it doesn't matter how well you do it.
3. If people were overwhelmed by the multiple channels in which to advertise, then they had a mammoth opportunity for thought leadership. All they needed to do was go out into the market and announce themselves as the market leader in the world of advertising spend. By telling their potential clients that they would solve that problem for them by giving them valuable information on how best to spend their advertising money, they became problem solvers. Be a problem solver. Be a thought leader. Be the teacher

unto those who spend. Give them good, solid, valuable advice that will benefit them ... and you will become the logical choice for their spend, even if you *weren't* punting your own product.

I also pointed out to them that there was no end to the number of media opportunities available for a big-name company like the *Yellow Pages*. They could tell potential customers "What has changed in advertising since the recession? This is how you can go about advertising intelligently today."

They could place articles on that topic. Appear on radio and television talk shows. Just recommend it to the right people. And they will give you the floor.

If enough of the right people see your message, you will experience the shift from pie man to guru. You will find that *they* start coming to *you*.

And that's a nice situation to be in!

Sometimes it's not about your sales techniques. Sometimes it's about thought leadership. Sometimes all you really need to do is position yourself as an expert.

## "YIKES! I CAN'T BE AN EXPERT! WHY, I'M NO MORE THAN A TERRIFIED MARSHMALLOW ...!"

Ah, yes. Fear. That cold, coppery-taste-in-the-mouth enemy that prevents us from doing so many things with our lives. Fear can be a significant obstacle to expert positioning because the status of "industry expert" seems lofty and unattainable.

You might be thinking, "Who am I to proclaim myself an expert?" And some attendant scary thoughts run through your mind, including:

- I'm just an upstart; no one's ever heard of me.
- I'd have to tell people what to do; why would they listen?
- I'd have to have something valuable to say.
- Imagine if I start positioning myself as an expert and they simply laugh at me?

Fear not. All these issues will be addressed well before you arrive on the mountainside. Consider this:

I grew up in a school system that promoted prefects among the senior children, a quintessentially British idea. As a high school student, I was equally excited and terrified about the prospect of some day becoming a prefect. I can remember standing in line at assembly, at about the age of 14, and looking at the kids all around me. They were taller, older, more confident, and I can actually remember the moment when I thought to myself, "How on earth could I ever tell them what to do?!"

It sounds silly now, but the idea kept me up at night. I desperately wanted to be a school prefect. But I spent years developing stomach aches about what might happen if I actually succeeded. As a small example, how would I tell another kid to tuck in the shirt of his uniform? They would just laugh at me!

Of course, I missed the glaringly obvious: by the time you arrive, you're older than the other kids. And for this reason, the balance of power shifts.

The same is true of your journey towards positioning yourself as an expert: *you will know what you're doing by the time you get there.* For now, it's enough that you *desire* to get there.

Don't fear the destination. Don't fear being underqualified by the time you arrive. The journey itself will equip you. In large part, this book will equip you. But you must start out with the *yearning*, the deep, driving desire to become something significant. The answers will come as you grow and learn. Your reputation will grow and flourish around you as you strive. And by the time you get to the mountainside, you will have acquired agility in your field, mastery of your facts and ideas, a sense of how to preside over your industry, and the respect of key players.

It is one of life's wonderful surprises that after being involved in the struggle for a number of years, one day you discover that you actually do have the answers.

So take heart. When the moment comes, you'll simply tell that kid to tuck in his shirt. And guess what? He'll do it.

**"WHAT IF EVERYONE DECIDES TO BE AN EXPERT?"**

Fear not. They won't.

Firstly, you're the one holding this book. This means that you are at least considering developing a conscious plan to become formidable. You're already ahead of 90% of the game. Most people are deliriously happy simply to coast and hope for the best.

Secondly, most people do not choose the high road. Or even if they do choose it, they do not stick to it with any considerable discipline. They become comfortable in their careers and rarely if ever will they consciously strive to enact a scenario change and become more.

Thirdly, geography creates regional experts. There may already be big names heading up your industry. But wherever you live, you can be the recognised expert where you are. Sure, there's a Donald Trump of property in New York. But as a property mogul in Johannesburg, he's not your competition, is he?

This is not to say that you can't be the foremost international expert, the very tip of the arrow, *Trump himself*. After all, someone has to be the world's foremost name, and frankly, why shouldn't it be you?

## THE PATH

And so, here is the essential transition that you will follow, from raw amateur to masterful guru. Naturally, your unique story may differ slightly in order, but it will look basically like this:

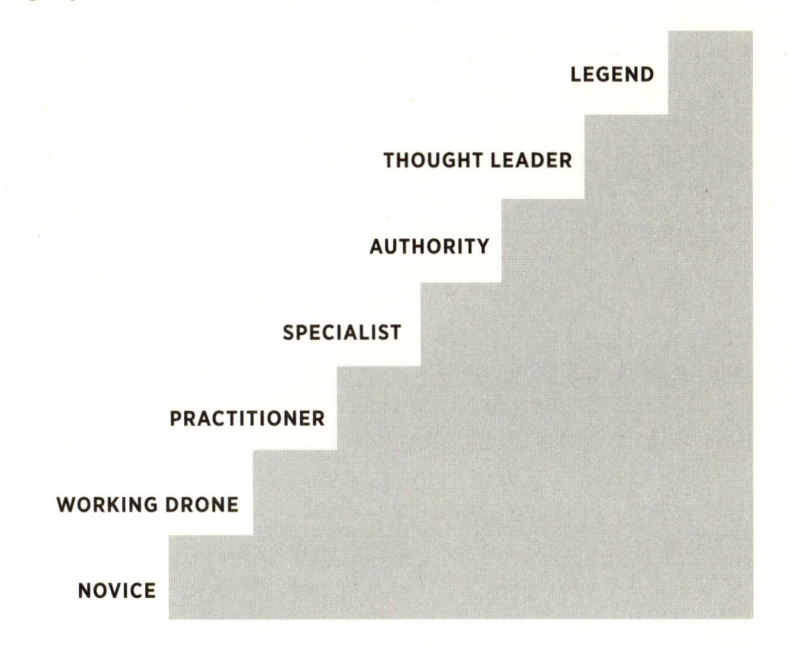

**LEGEND**
**THOUGHT LEADER**
**AUTHORITY**
**SPECIALIST**
**PRACTITIONER**
**WORKING DRONE**
**NOVICE**

Where would you place yourself on this scale right now? Your job is to move to higher levels by conscious design. In a bit more detail, here are the stages that you will go through:

## NOVICE

This level starts with basic learning. You go to school, you get an education, you're introduced into your industry. Finding the right industry may take a number of years as you dabble in and then leave different vocations, before finding the one that captures your interest.

## WORKING DRONE

You're employed. You develop competence. You start to feel comfortable with your tasks at work. At this stage, however, you are still reactively taking orders. You know what to do because you are told what to do.

## PRACTITIONER

You've realised that there is a wider world to your industry, and you've started to network. You read industry publications, go to events, meet others and explore the universe of your industry. You compare your views, knowledge and production to that of others because your performance is beginning to matter to you. It's no longer just about the tasks you do. You are starting to see a bigger picture.

## SPECIALIST

You're displaying initiative. Thinking critically. You can see what should be done, and you don't need to ask others how and when to do it. You start to make things happen, of your own accord because you know it needs to be done and you are the person to do it. You are developing passion for what you do. You no longer require the guidance, or possibly even the employment, of others. You are heading up your own work and initiating your own projects. You understand enough about your industry to operate independently in it.

## AUTHORITY

You are developing a reputation. You are becoming known as a formidable figure in industry circles. You are seen at events, requested as a speaker, sought after for articles and ideas. The key players in your industry know who you are and you are recommended. You are becoming the answer to the question, "You know who you should talk to?"

    Your work has also developed a unique signature. You have moved beyond mere independence. You are pioneering. You've found *better* ways of doing things. You're able to be artistic about what you do, rather than merely functional. You find ways of doing it that are uniquely *you*; your work bears your recognisable flourish; and you are becoming iconic as a result.

**THOUGHT LEADER**

You are exerting the beginnings of control over and influence in your industry. You are now at such a level of mastery and expertise that the industry looks to you for guidance. You are strongly opinionated, and no longer need the approval of others. You don't play by expected rules; you determine them. You are the thought leader at conferences, because you know – and can teach others – how things *should* be. You are a voice and an authority.

**LEGEND**

You have attained iconic status. You've been doing it so long, so brilliantly, and with such consistency, that your name is lauded and remembered even after you are gone. Others strive to emulate you as the gold standard. Your name is indelibly etched upon the consciousness of your industry. You are the Babe Ruth of your ball game, the Spielberg of your space, the Stephen King of your craft.

So, where do you find yourself right now? Do you have a number of these qualities and accomplishments under your belt yet? Chances are that if you've bought this book, you've probably already discovered some degree of enjoyment in what you do, and you desire to become more. You see the value in further education and aspiration in your industry.

If you're still new to it all, no matter. Let's get started with building your expertise and your reputation.

# WHICH PHILOSOPHY?

Let's deal with some thoughts on what this book is *not* about. It is not about transforming you into some sombre, suit-wearing banker type. It's not about making you a more serious person. On the contrary, some of the most successful experts are eccentric, off-the-wall, larger-than-life characters who stand out in their industries.

In fact, this book does not give you your philosophy. It merely points out that you should have one. It doesn't set your marketing tone. It simply offers you ways and means to express that tone. It doesn't tell you what to *be*. Only how to be *that* more effectively.

I will not try to prescribe the right type of personality to set you apart; that would make you inauthentic. I will merely point out the importance of bringing personality to the mix, for knowledge alone, you will discover, is not enough.

So take comfort. I have no intention of changing you. I only want to make you a more pronounced and effective version of yourself. I don't want to alter your handwriting. I just want to backlight your signature and put it up in lights.

I will say this much, though. You must feel a sense of yearning for greatness for this process to work. What *type* of greatness is your kettle of fish, and the nature of your ultimate success is really whatever blows your hair back. But *yearning* ...! It must be there. As Jon Bon Jovi observed:

I think any kid who picks up a guitar should only ever think that he's going to be Mick Jagger. Not "I want to be the opening act for Jagger." No. I want to be Mick F*n Jagger!

I want you to desire to be the best. If you can meet me at that starting point, we can work together.

# WHAT IT WILL TAKE TO DESIGN "YOU"

I believe that experts exist at the intersection of three elements. They are:

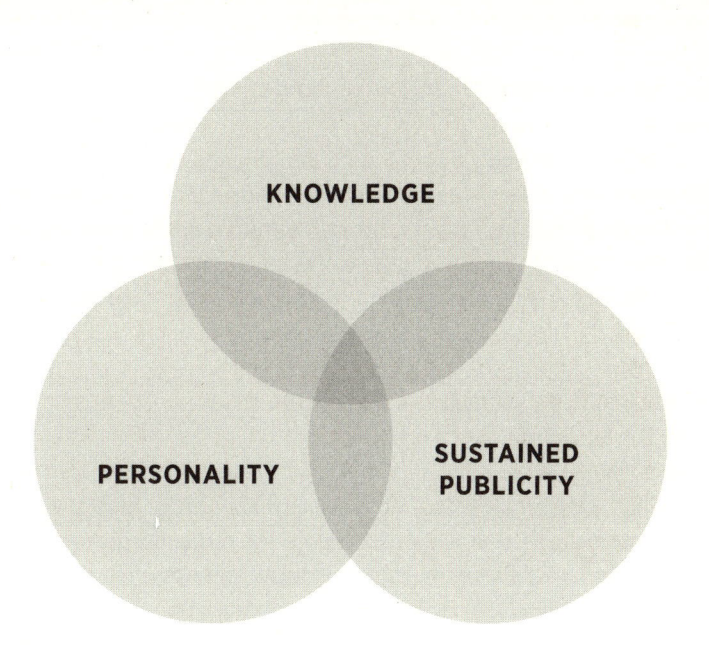

KNOWLEDGE

PERSONALITY

SUSTAINED PUBLICITY

Take any one of these three out of the mix, and you no longer have an expert. They are non-negotiable. Let me explain:

**ALL THE KNOWLEDGE WITHOUT THE PERSONALITY**

Every large organisation has one of these individuals. You'll usually find him down in the third-level basement. His office is behind a rusted old car, inside a door marked "No hawkers". Once you open the door, you generally have to kick a pizza box out of the way, brush aside a cobweb, and search the musky, darkened room for signs of life.

... And you'll find them towards the back of the room, crouching behind a filing cabinet, staring at you with crazed eyes like Gollum in *The Lord of the Rings*.

This is the man who knows everything there is to know about the systems that run this organisation. He has all the technical knowledge in the world ... but he is completely unable to converse with human beings. He doesn't seem to blink often enough. He's often an IT specialist.

All the knowledge in the world has not created the perception of an expert, nor will he be remunerated like one. The Personality and Publicity are missing.

### ALL THE PERSONALITY, BUT NO KNOWLEDGE

If you have all the knowledge, but no personality, you are a specialist. If you have all the personality, but no knowledge, you are a Kardashian.

So a question for you to consider at this point in your career is this: are you currently the dusty professor or the curvy Kardashian? They exist at opposing ends of the scale, and you actually need a little bit of both.

### KNOWLEDGE, PERSONALITY AND PUBLICITY

"Expert" is a perception. It is a socially created and agreed upon idea. And to create a perception, you must show your face, they must hear your voice, read your words, *encounter* you and experience you. You cannot be an expert by remote control. You have to go out and intentionally publicise your knowledge and your personality.

Working on these three will ultimately position you as an expert in your industry. You may ask:

- "What if I'm not naturally loud and charismatic?"
- "What if I'm a little short on industry knowledge?"
- "What if I don't know how to publicise myself, or feel uncomfortable or ignoble doing so?"

You don't have to change your personality. There are some highly successful, softly spoken and introverted experts in many industries. You simply need to publicise *your* personality – your unique, thumb-print identity, even if it's a quiet, calm one.

In terms of gathering the knowledge and insight, I'll show you how to do this in the next few pages. And in terms of publicising yourself, I'll give you useful, practical and fairly simple ways to go about it. i am not trying to turn you into a circus show. The idea is simply to take your personality and your expertise on tour.

It's not an act of quantum physics to align personality, knowledge and sustained publicity. It just takes dedication and some honest hard work. It all begins with the desire to do so on purpose.

On that note, I want to be clear that positioning yourself as an expert will take time. It will also take mental energy, discipline, and sustained activity. It isn't going to happen overnight, but instead will be the sum total of your sustained thoughts and actions over time. Sometimes quite a substantial amount of time.

In my own case, it required around eight years of active positioning before the BMWs and Microsofts of the world started to call me, and I started to feel that I'd finally "arrived". Sure, I had enjoyed many small successes (and plenty of failures!) along the way. But that *tipping point*, as Malcolm Gladwell would put it, was a long time in the making.

This book won't replace hard work. But it will show you how to aim your hard work in the right direction. It will shorten your learning curve, and get you doing the right things sooner in your career.

Think of it in the same way as going to a gym. You can walk into a gym and spend an hour doing all the wrong things. Day by day, you could expend huge amounts of energy doing exercises that won't get you the results you desire. You want big muscles. But cardio doesn't seem to be helping. If only somebody had told you that you need to lift heavy weights instead!

I will be that person. I would like to show you how to accelerate your growth curve and aim your energies in the right direction.

Becoming an expert will also take a lot of self-promotion on your part. US speaker and consultant, Alan Weiss, often says that unless you're blowing your own horn, there is no music. Positioning yourself means promoting yourself, although it need not be shamelessly.

If this doesn't seem natural to you, or if it feels contrary to the manners and modesty you were taught as a child, don't worry.

I'm not asking you to become a used-car salesman with a Cheshire cat grin and a megaphone. You may, if you wish, choose to position yourself as a quiet, intellectual kind of expert. That's good too. I'll just show you how to get your message, your brand and your image *out there*. After all, an expert is not an expert in isolation. The very term implies the consensus of others. Expert is a public perception.

Ready to get started?

Great! Let's jump right into the practical things that you can do in order to manage how others perceive you.

Here are 50 ways to position yourself as an expert ...

# THE CULTURE OF LIVING AS AN EXPERT

**THE DAILY DIFFERENCE**

You can imagine that sustaining a career as an industry expert takes a great deal of focus. The basic attitude is different for starters. You certainly can't live as haphazardly as people in your industry who have simply stumbled into careers and progressed by the slow march of time, rather than by design or effort. Being an expert requires a great deal of focused personal discipline.

You're not just in it because your parents told you to be. You're in it because you love it!

But it's not just about focus, discipline and hard work. There is also a fundamental shift in the way that you carry out your work. Let us use the example of an entry-level salesperson versus a highly focused expert consultant. Let's assume, for the purpose of illustration, that the salesperson got his job because it was the only thing available, not because he had a passion for sales and studied the craft like an expert. Now, let's assume that the consultant is representative of what an expert should be on a daily basis, and compare the two.

**PROBLEMS**
CREATE INDUSTRY

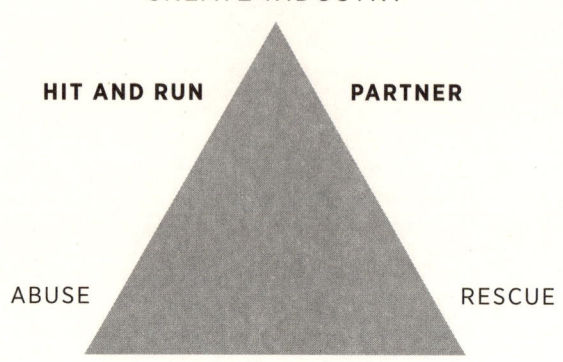

HIT AND RUN — PARTNER

ABUSE — RESCUE

The low-level salesperson practises hit and run. He is willing to abuse to get what he wants. The high-level consultant genuinely cares about solving the problems of his clientele. He will actually turn work away if he feels he can't provide genuine value.

In the course of this book, I will give you some practical ways to enhance the public's perception of you. But nothing – I repeat, *nothing* – is more important than this one principle: you must care about what you do.

If you take your work seriously and care deeply about what you do, the chances are that you will eventually end up as an industry expert, even without the assistance of these ideas. But if you don't care about your industry, no amount of strategic input will ever get you there.

Experts have a different culture to low-level workers. They think about their industry, fixate on it, care about it, worry about it, wish they could change it, speak to it, interact with it, affect it and assist in growing it. Their love of it is palpable, and that is already most of the battle won. One of the surest ways to win any contest is to out-care your competition.

You can fake a great many things in life. But you can't fool yourself into a 40-year career as an expert in an industry you don't care about.

# 50 WAYS TO POSITION YOURSELF AS AN EXPERT

# 1. UNDERSTAND THE SCIENCE OF TALENT

All things begin with attitude. For this reason, I don't want you to decide to be *good* at what you do. I would like you to decide from the outset to be the very best.

Performance specialists, from the sports to the business arena, will tell you that deciding to be "good" is not nearly as effective as deciding to be "the best". There is a vast psychological difference between the two, and it will affect your performance.

If you plan to take your career seriously, and be recognised as pre-eminent, you need to make this decision early on. Deciding to be "good" allows you a great deal of leeway, but deciding to be the very best demands much more of you. It demands higher-level thinking and more intense levels of research, practice and performance.

Let the feel-good speakers and authors tell you about *all things in moderation* ... But the reality is that if you want to be an expert, you actually need to obsess about what you do. You need to demand great things of yourself. Obsession is a powerful thing.

In fact, it forms the basis of what is now considered to be the accepted formula for developing talent in any field.

Talent, it turns out, is neither inborn nor genetic. The latest research reveals that there is a formula, which, if followed, can take you to master levels of performance in your sphere. To develop talent – in anything – you need all the constituent parts in this formula:

**TALENT = Yearning + Input + Deliberate Practice, Sustained**

That's it; the whole enchilada. And it applies to anything.

This formula is the result of decades of international study into the topic of Talent, and is admirably explored in Malcolm Gladwell's book, *Outliers*, as well as Geoff Colvin's *Talent is Overrated*.

**THE TALENT EQUATION**

Let's start with Yearning. You have to want to learn. If you have no desire to improve, no burning need to be great at what you do, the other factors will remain irrelevant in a "horse to the water" sort of way. But if you do have even the slightest inkling for betterment, you're already at a distinct advantage over those who do not. Now you will need the next factor: Input.

Input means any form of teaching or coaching. Simply put, you need someone to show you how. If you have yearning but no input, your development can only progress so far, and it will be slow in coming.

Reading is one form of input, and it's a good one, but it is important to note that self-teaching is not nearly as effective as having another person coach you, particularly in the early stages of developing proficiency in a new field. Master practitioners may know enough about their fields to coach themselves, but starting out, we don't know what we don't know. For this reason, external input is very valuable.

**THE MOST IMPORTANT INGREDIENT**

The next factor is the most important of all: Deliberate Practice. This is vastly different to what most people have in mind when they think of practice. Deliberate Practice occurs when you break a thing down into its constituent parts, and then work on getting better at each part in isolation. You achieve this only through mind-numbing amounts of repetition, with a focus on improving each element in isolation.

It explains why some people can put in the fabled 10 000 hours of practice playing golf, and not improve one jot, while others will soar to the professional ranks with the same amount of time. The difference lies in *how* they practise.

An average golfer, for instance, will spend x amount of time playing a round of golf. The yearning may be present, but there is no outside input and no Deliberate Practice. Just generic golfing. Hence, his time teaches him almost nothing.

A great golfer, however, will spend the same number of hours practising precisely *how to get a ball out of a sand bunker*. He focuses on just this one element, and does it over and over, thus improving one constituent part of his total game. He then moves on to another part. And this is Deliberate Practice. He may even do it in conjunction with the input of a coach, which would greatly enhance his efficacy.

And this is why most people will never get better at practices like public speaking, despite a lifetime of giving presentations at work. They are not improving the constituent parts of their speaking abilities. Moreover, they receive little to no coaching or constructive feedback. They are merely "playing a game of golf". Furthermore, they are generally traumatised by each instance, which reduces their capacity for the very first element in the Talent equation: Yearning. Because they fear it, they don't want to learn how to do it better.

So, armed with this knowledge, how exactly do you ensure that you become a master practitioner at what you do? The answer is relatively simple although the work that it entails is not. You need to break it down into its constituent parts, and then find ways to practise and perfect each part.

Let's use public speaking as an example.

I have an exercise that I use when training executives, and you can try it for yourself. Initially, it looks and feels rather ridiculous. But the more time we spend in a training room doing it, the more the benefit becomes apparent to my trainees.

I get them to stand in front of a room, as though poised to deliver a speech. But this is where things get abstract: instead of speaking, they have to count. They have to count using different emotions, and at different speeds and volumes, as though they were giving the greatest oratory performance in the history of public speaking, with every shade and nuance of feeling, even though all they are saying is, "1, 2, 3, 4, 5 ... !"

Why? Well, firstly, because it renders some surprisingly humorous results for me as the coach.

But secondly, and more importantly, because it allows them to practise the *parts* of public speaking without having to think about the *words*. I take intellectual content out of the equation, I take fear of speaking out of the equation and I get them to focus only on the rhythms and physical movements of speaking. In this way they can concentrate on improving what they do with their hands; how they stand and move; how to use their voices; how to create emphasis and emotion; pausing; playing with facial expressions; and so on.

It's like a musician practising scales on a piano. In fact, I call it "the scales of public speaking".

Having coached them through this process, I then assign homework. My delegates must spend a certain amount of time in front of a mirror at home (preferably in private as families have a way of doubling over with laughter), and simply go through the motions over and over, until they actually approve of the rhythms and patterns they see in the mirror.

Then, once they are back in front of a live audience and they replace the numbers with content, the deeply ingrained muscle-memory kicks in, and the grace is naturally there.

Deliberate Practice. Break down and rebuild. It's the single greatest distinction between amateurs and super-performers.

## DANGER ZONE!

Here is an interesting and counter-intuitive point about Talent. When it starts coming naturally and automatically, you have hit your first Talent Cap. You have arrived at a developmental ceiling.

This happens in a very obvious way with driving. When your average driver gets to the point where it "comes without thinking", he has hit his performance potential and will generally not improve further over the course of a lifetime. Sometimes, he will even get slightly worse, year by year.

So, is it possible to break through such a performance barrier and achieve the next level of performance? Yes. But only consciously. You have to identify the ceiling – realise that you have reached a level of automatic proficiency – and then overcome it by design. Otherwise, it will simply never happen.

Using the car example, once you've reached automatic proficiency and realised it, you could then do an advanced driving course, which pushes you beyond your comfort zone, or perhaps learn some new, daring stunts involving a car (just not in my neighbourhood, please).

This forces you to think about your craft again, and to learn by conscious design instead of repeating apathetically.

If you identify and use this simple principle, your performance potential – in any sphere – will be leagues ahead of most.

Obsessing about your field is important, and obsession is a powerful force. If you'd like to see this sort of obsession in practice and what it can achieve, take a look at a man who was arguably the greatest performer of the last century: Michael Jackson. It's no coincidence that people still use terms like "legendary", "greatest" and "king of …" when they talk about him.

The movie *This is It!* features footage from rehearsals prior to what would have been Jackson's final tour, but for his untimely death. In it we see the incredible level of demand he placed upon himself and the kind of exacting standards he expected from his co-performers. There is absolutely no sense of "It will do" in his approach. Not even in the smallest details. The King of Pop wanted absolutely everything to be done in the absolutely best way possible.

Again: *obsession*. There are few things more powerful.

So, whether your goal is to become the highest paid consultant in your industry, or the most renowned creative mind in your field, or the grand high-lama of flower arrangers, this is your first step: decide that you want to be the very best. Obsess about it. Break it down into its smallest constituent parts. Tune your mind to it, seek input, use deliberate practice, and you will start assimilating the information and performance cues necessary to make it happen.

Don't aim for good. Aim for "the greatest".

**Key question:**
Have you made the decision to be at the top of your game?

## 2. DETERMINE YOUR VALUES

This book is about promoting who you are. So ... who are you?

It's an extremely valuable exercise for you to start this process by seriously asking yourself this question. I'd even encourage you to put this book down at the end of this chapter and to mull this one over for a while. Whether you like to gaze at the stars, or take long walks when you're thinking, whether your best thinking happens on a gym treadmill or on a long drive, go and do that thing. Programme your mind to answer this question while you do: Who are you? Who do you want to be? How do you want to be seen in ten years' time?

Why would you invest so much time in such a seemingly vague exercise? The answer is: because you are designing the rest of your life. Expert Positioning is a lot of work. And the outcome will be the story of your time on this planet. It's that important.

When you've had a little time to dream and imagine, get a piece of paper and write down some notes. Nothing too complicated. Just a few thoughts on who you believe you are, who you want to be and what you stand for.

To draw from the world of expert chefs, are you the Jamie Oliver of your industry: a down-to-earth and kind-hearted bloke-next-door? Or are you more of a hard-driving Gordon Ramsay type? Are you an Oprah? Or a Jerry Springer? Teacher, counsellor, performer, or maverick? All are models for leading lights in an industry.

To get at the most accurate possible answer, ask yourself what you like in your current idols. And what you abhor in celebrities whom you don't want to emulate. Ask yourself whether you are naturally already an extroverted, controversial type, or whether you're more of the quiet specialist.

Write down who you are, and then write down who you want to be in an ideal world.

Because we're dealing with an ideal version of you, feel free to exaggerate. You can intentionally overstate your good qualities. If you feel you're good at networking, write down: "The most effective social networker in the industry". If you're highly productive, write down: "A constantly producing human *machine*! People just can't understand how I could have such a fertile mind! Creator of worlds and crafter of intellectual universes!"

Or perhaps: "She's so very wise. We all run about like chickens without heads, but she's like an oasis of calm wisdom and dependable guidance."

Go to town. Feel free to inspire yourself to become more of what you currently value in yourself or in your idols. After all, you need the *yearning.* Yearning comes with thinking about how much and how formidable you could be.

Next, consider this: what will be unique about you *when* you are an expert? What will make you distinctive? Who will you be? Will you have the risqué sensuality of a Nigella Lawson? Or the powerful command of someone whose image is bone-dry intellectual?

Go ahead and do that now. Get a good handle on what type of expert you want to be; what type of person you see yourself growing into. Present yourself back inside these pages once you're done ...

**Key question:**
What do you want to stand for?

# 3. OUTWORK THE COMPETITION

Working smart has always been deemed better than working hard. I have no argument. But a true professional understands that working smart is not a *replacement* for working hard. You need the two together. Their cumulative effect on your career over time can be massive.

At a Toastmasters conference at which I was asked to present, I made the remark that the real secret to winning the SA Championships five times was simply w*anting it* more than my competitors (this, again, is the Yearning part of the Talent equation). I believe that I won the contest repeatedly for a very simple reason: I consistently chose to outwork the competition (and this is the Deliberate Practice part).

While the other speakers put hours into honing a script, and hours more into practising its delivery, I invested weeks into honing my script, and months into improving my delivery. With that much work and dedication, *anyone* could take the trophy. The only difference was that I actually did put in those hours. It's worth noting that I also placed a big emphasis on external mentoring or coaching, which fulfils the Input aspect of the Talent equation.

This approach is a universal recipe for success, applicable to any industry. And while we're on the topic of wanting more and working hard to get it, here's an interesting point to consider:

**COMPLACENCY, NOT HARDSHIP, IS THE ENEMY OF ACCOMPLISHMENT.**

You may have heard the catchphrase "Good is the enemy of great". There's a lot of truth in this sentiment. People tend to reach a certain level of performance competence, and hence, "comfort" at work. And it's fact that because they are "good" at something, this actually holds them back from becoming truly great. They settle for good. The pay is nice and they start to coast. Good becomes good enough.

People who are good are not hungry. People who are good are not desperate. People who are good are not eager to prove themselves. They plateau. And there is no outside force to compel them to become more.

Your compelling force, therefore, must come from the inside, and this is why you must make the decision to be the very best, and not merely good at what you do.

Greatness is born of discomfort and dissatisfaction with your status quo. And it can be extremely difficult to make yourself unhappy with your status quo when you're comfortable and relatively well off.

Top bodybuilders know it. Just take a look at any muscle magazine. A surprising quantity of editorial is dedicated to encouraging practitioners to be discontent with their current physique, unhappy with their levels of performance and dissatisfied with their capacity to lift weights. They contend that the less you allow yourself to settle for what you have, the less willing you'll be to accept performance plateaus and the more you will strive for more.

Dissatisfaction with your own performance is actually a kind of mental discipline. And it's a recipe for true greatness.

Work hard. But let's not forget the second part of that formula. Work smart as well.

Classic hamster thinking – *employee*-level thinking – says you should just keep your head down and run on that treadmill, and eventually you'll get somewhere.

Well, you might, ultimately, but it will be a long, slow and frankly stupid curve. And you will not reach the heights possible with a combination of hard work and clever strategy.

People who try to grow their career with hard work only are missing the personality component of expert positioning. How many people do you know who work incredibly hard, but have never become more than, say, a secretary at their organisation? They complain that they are not promoted in spite of how hard they work. I contend that hard work has little to do with it. In simple language, they are not spectacular enough. They are not leaders, speakers, growers, big personas. They have failed to grow the Personality part of the expert equation, and no amount of hard work will get them over their plateau.

If you really want to be the best in your industry, make it your goal to advance quickly. Out-work your competitors. Out-think them.

Spend time and energy on the body of work that your industry entails, but don't neglect to spend equal amounts of energy on thinking constructively and strategically outside the actual work itself. Lift your head from the murk and look around you. Think about your career. Think about your persona and your presence. Think about what your next step is. Learn to want it more than anyone else. Above all, stay hungry.

**Key question:**
Are you hungrier than your peers and competitors?

## 4. START ASKING "THE CONSTANT QUESTION"

This is a principle I use in my training, and in my own personal development, and it works exceptionally well. The psychology is this: if you think about the colour red, for example, you'll start to notice red everywhere. Think about your favourite make of car, and suddenly you'll become aware of how many of them are on the roads. The more you fixate on something, the more you notice it everywhere. You 'tune in' to it.

You can use this principle in positioning yourself as an expert. Let me use an example from my training in presentation skills ...

The best speakers and presenters are the ones who are acutely aware of "effect". They are fascinated by how you achieve effects that audiences like and respond to. They will watch other people's speeches – both the good and the bad – and ask themselves, "Why did that work?" or "Why didn't it?" They are hard-core students of effect. They are tuned in to it. They are always looking for the colour red and so they see it everywhere. It's as though they've tuned their receptors into this particular area and so the information that is useful and valuable to them just floods in.

The best speakers don't just do it with speeches either. They'll gather useful information about "creating effect" from all sorts of sources. This includes reading, watching shows on TV, listening to music, viewing ice-skating – just about anything that has an element of artistic output. They are constantly asking questions about what works and why; what doesn't and why not.

This principle will work for you as you begin to position yourself as an expert, regardless of your field.

In everything you see, ask yourself: Did I believe it? Or not? Am I impressed by that approach? Or did it fail? Did it create authority? Or was it lame? Did that article jump out at me as the work of an expert? Or the fumbling of an amateur? Was it credible? Or did it fall short? What works and what doesn't?

Asking yourself "The Constant Question" will help you to become *familiar* with excellence in your field.

Psychologists know that when you are constantly fixating on a topic or idea, the information pertaining to that topic will jump out at you from all sides. Fixate on the idea of being an expert and the world is your classroom!

**Key question:**
Are you constantly looking for information on how to become more?

## 5. DEVOUR KNOWLEDGE

Knowledge is power. So how do you consume sufficient amounts of the stuff to become an expert?

After all, you can't position yourself as an expert unless you possess a formidable body of knowledge concerning your industry. It is one part of your big three: Knowledge, Personality and Sustained Publicity. The last thing you want is to elevate yourself successfully to the position of a perceived expert, only to be caught with your pants down in the knowledge department when it really matters.

Imagine, for instance, being hired by a large firm which has identified you as the person to address their problem, only to embarrass yourself by not knowing obvious terminology. Or not being able to answer a question because you don't truly understand what they are asking. Chances are, you'll never work for that company again, and your future in the industry may be in jeopardy.

You need the knowledge. You need the experience. And that means that you have to put in the hours.

So, here is a simple formula for acquiring it, courtesy of US motivational speaker, Earl Nightingale (1921– 1989):

**Study your topic for one hour each day.**

If you spend just one hour daily reading and thinking about your industry, within one year, you will be an expert on the topic. In fact, if you *genuinely* spend that much time reading up on your topic, you'd probably be a national expert. One hour a day adds up dramatically over time.

In *Outliers*, mentioned earlier, Malcolm Gladwell explains that it takes 10 000 hours to become an international master at just about anything. This may seem daunting, but it's worth remembering that with 1 000 or 2 000 hours, you can become exceptionally good. 10 000 hours is master-class level. It's the level of experience that creates Mozarts and Tiger Woodses. And it will come eventually. You just need to get started with your first thousand. It's enough to focus on that for now.

What is your source for this knowledge? Your reading may be informed by useful websites, ezines, books or newspapers. It may be more practical in nature, as you actually *do* what your industry entails, learning by experience. Personally, I like to devour books. I have also found that downloadable audio books assist me in getting to knowledge when I am driving or lack the time to read.

Effective learning comes with a certain attitude, though. It's the difference between a person who does by rote, and one who is genuinely interested in becoming better. After all, you can coast in an industry for 40 years, doing but never growing. Or you can become formidable in it within five. The difference is in your attitude to learning.

If you yearn for greatness, you will constantly seek ways to improve. You will study your craft, study the best, read the guides, seek counsel and question the established wisdom. You will want to know and, in many instances, you will disagree with the answers you receive, or feel that they are not complete. You will be in constant journey mode, ever seeking more.

And so, you need both practice and input. Don't just do by rote without input. Practise and read. Do and study. Work and learn.

If you're serious about what you do, and if you love your industry enough to become an expert in it, put in the time. Know thy content!

**Key question:**
Do you know where to source sufficient reading materials on your topic to fuel an hour of reading each day?

## 6. FIND A NICHE

International speaker Joe Calloway calls it "Becoming a category of one". Other speakers, pronouncing the word in the US manner, cite the catchphrase "There are riches in niches".

The more focused your field of expertise is, the easier it is to position yourself as an expert. The more strongly you are associated with a specific field, endeavour or idea, the more you begin to own that part of the industry in the public's eyes.

Be specific and find your niche. In other words, don't be a broad-based generalist. Be a specialist. Go for depth, not breadth.

People are not inspired by a general practitioner who covers a broad range of generic topic matter; the old "I can do a bit of everything" approach. It smacks of the low-level worker who is desperate for any job and willing to shuffle by with a little bit of this and a little bit of that. The more focused you are, and the more pinpoint your area of expertise, the more impressive and specialised you appear. And appearances, after all, are a formidable part of Expert Positioning.

It's the difference between a journalist and a *political* journalist, a trainer or a *sales* trainer, or even a sales trainer who focuses specifically on closing large deals with multinational companies. It's the archaeologist versus the third-dynasty Egyptologist.

Being part of a general field is a good start, but bear in mind it's only a start. To become an expert, you must be seen as something more specific in that field.

And it's amazing just how specific you can be if you're willing to put some thought into it. One US speaker, author and trainer, has made a career by targeting the military circuit, using the topic "Military

Deployment Separation Issues". She speaks and trains on how to cope when family members are deployed to war zones. She's even developed unique products to sell to her market. This is remarkably specific.

When no one else speaks, trains or writes on such a topic, suddenly you will find yourself owning that space. And when the topic arises, people say, "You know who you should talk to?" Tagging your name to the end of that sentence in the public consciousness is the heart and soul of expert positioning.

Another international speaker, Dale Irvin, bills himself as a "Professional Summariser". He attends meetings and conventions and provides humorous summaries of the events, speakers and topics. Just that. Where is the value in this positioning? Well, convention planners know that their delegates will stay until the end of the event because they know that's when the funny part will be. This makes him valuable. He's the guy you go to if you want to achieve *that*.

Curiously, narrowing your field down to an area of specific interest will *not* usually limit your customer base. Ironically, it tends to *increase* it. This is because the more specific an entity you are, the more easily you stand out as the go-to person for that topic. Not only that, but you'll also inspire greater confidence in your customer base. Observe the difference:

*Generalist:* I teach customer service skills.
*Specialist:* I teach eight ways to keep your big accounts during a recession.

Or again:

*Generalist:* I do motivational talks for companies.
*Specialist:* I speak on future trends and how companies can exploit them ahead of their competitors.

Interestingly, your choice of niche will also determine your business model. Some businesses have to rely heavily on advertising. Others get business almost exclusively from referrals. Everyone's scenario is different, and choosing a niche will actually determine your business model. You will need to go about marketing and advertising yourself according to what works best for your target market. A specialist in the farming industry will have a completely different business model to someone in insurance.

The good news is that the more specific and developed your niche is, the more people will get to know you, and the less you'll need to do in the way of advertising as you become "the logical choice".

There is a wonderful snowball effect that occurs when you position yourself cleverly as a well-niched expert. Some experts so utterly own their industries that they don't need to advertise at all. The work just comes to them, and often in greater volumes than they can manage.

What a wonderful problem to have!

(Actually, it is a problem to have, and we will discuss how you can handle it when we look at your pricing model.)

Another interesting by-product of focusing on a niche is that your followers tend to become devotees. Usually, when people are interested in your topic, they are *very* interested in it, and they'll devour any literature or thought-leadership materials you produce. They'll follow you on social networks and seek you out for their events. If you provide exactly what they are looking for, they'll keep on coming to you for more.

I began to experience this phenomenon when an organisation said, "We enjoyed your speech and your books. Do you have anything more? Maybe a DVD or two?" Devotees will buy everything you have, and they alone can double or triple your income. Provided you have been clever enough to make the products they crave. But we'll get to that in the next chapter.

**Key question:**
Are you prostituting yourself by doing a little bit of everything, or have you found your area of focus?

## 7. BE A PRODUCER

*If they love you, they will want more of what you do. If you create it, they will buy it. If you build it, they will come.*

In the realm of professional speakers, who are all essentially performing content experts, it's surprising to see how many of those billing themselves as "professional" are simply not *producers*. They are performers, yes, with a single keynote presentation, but they often get stuck in time and cease to produce.

They don't create articles, they don't write books, they don't come up with new ideas on purpose and they don't design or conceive anything new. They stop contributing. They may very well be specialists in their field, but people tend to forget them because they are not constantly innovating, not constantly putting out into the world; and this changes their role from thought leaders to mere performers.

These closed factories generally do not prosper to the same extent as experts whose mental factory lights are always blazing, whose idea-production lines are always running, who are ruthlessly industrious and constantly "putting out into the world".

And they fail to prosper for two reasons:

1. Production means more sales – if you offer them more, and they buy more, you can double or triple your income.
2. Production keeps you visible – the more you produce, the more opportunities you have for visibility in your industry.

There's a phrase written by an author from the previous century, James A. Michener, that I find inspiring. He recalls a period in his life when he was writing over 7 000 words a day. He described this act as an "almost indecent display of industry". The phrasing of this statement hits the spot for me.

James A. Michener was seen, worldwide, as *the* foremost author of historical fiction and a mind to be reckoned with. And just like Stephen King, who is often lauded as the bestselling living author today, Michener ascribed his astonishingly high-level reputation to honest hard work. Lots of it. He was a constant producer.

Imagine if James A. Michener or Stephen King had written what they considered to be their "one great novel" and then stopped there. Picture Stephen King writing *Carrie*, then sitting back in his chair and declaring, "Right! I'm done. People should hand me a career now."

It may have even worked. For one year. After that, no one would remember who Stephen King was. And yet, 40 years later, he remains at the top of the bestseller lists simply because he is a producer.

Stephen King himself contends that one of the major differences between him and the average aspiring writer is sheer volume of output. It brings in (a lot of!) income for him, and it keeps him visible. Moreover, he has created worldwide tribes, who will buy anything he produces without question or evaluation, simply because it is the production of Stephen King. He is the guru on the hillside. The trusted voice. They go to him. They will have anything he will give. And they will pay handsomely for it. I know because I am one of them.

The "one great novel" approach would be equivalent to what many experts are trying to do today. It just doesn't work. You have to go on to novel number two. You have to, in Stephen King terms, get started on your *Salem's Lot*.

It's a constant gradient of productive output that ultimately adds up to a real career and has people recognising you as someone at the top of your game. And the more you produce, the more you are able to charge for what you produce. Stephen King's books cost more than those of entry-level authors simply because of the equity of his name. In the same way that your remuneration should not be calculated in hours, but rather in value, Stephen King's remuneration is not calculated in pages, but in equity of brand.

So, if you are an expert in flowers, when will you write a book on the topic? And what will the second book be about? And the third? What new things can you do around flowers? Is there some novel way to present them to your market? Is there a TV show that you could do about them (and preferably something a little cleverer and quirkier than just a gardening show)? Or perhaps a road show? What's the *next* big thing in flowers? Have you stamped your intellectual mark on it? When people think about flowers, why should they think about you?

Constant output is the key. It gives you publicity, it creates tribes, it raises the price of your product, it positions you as the guru, it keeps them coming back for more. Be a producer. It's one of the most important elements in positioning yourself as an expert.

If you're a financial adviser, write a small guide. When you're done, think of the next thing.

The more you produce, the more visibility you have. Each new article is an advert for you. Each presentation, interview or television appearance is a marketing campaign. Each new book is a quantum leap forward for your credibility. And every new *idea* positions you as a thinker and a leader and, quite simply, someone interesting within your sphere.

We will take a more specific look at the notions of book- and article-writing later on, but for now, it's worth just coming to terms with the idea that being a producer of some description is critically important. The more you produce, and the more interesting your ideas, the better it is for your career.

**Key question:**
When people think about your industry, why should they think about you?

# 8. BE A FACE AND A VOICE

Appearance is everything ... so appear!

I don't believe that it is critical what clothing you wear, what car you drive, or where you live. But I do believe that it is critical that they see your face and hear your voice. You have to be a human being who the market and the industry know, not a name on a piece of paper or a signature on an email.

With this in mind, here's a good idea: call the editor of the magazine that handles your industry and introduce yourself. Here's an even better idea: go around and meet her. Similarly, it's a good idea to send an email to an agent. It's a much better idea to take her to coffee and chat face to face.

Sales people call it "face time" and it's invaluable. It's one thing to be an expert on a piece of paper, but it's an entirely different proposition to become a known entity: a real human being with a personality in the minds of the key players.

When I started writing for a certain sales magazine, I made a point of dropping by their offices to introduce myself. There was no need: my articles had already been accepted for publication, but I went ahead and did it anyway. This was the beginning of a relationship that:

- grew my presence in the publication itself
- culminated in the staff recommending my services when people asked about professional speakers
- turned me into the preferred specialist when they had a publishing requirement relating to my field.

These sorts of encounters – simple in nature; you just drop by and say "hi" – can mean the difference between being an obscure name on a list and being seen as the go-to person. It's fairly logical. If you were a representative of experts, be it the editor of a publication who publishes their work, or an agent with a pool of performers, you'd be much more inclined to recommend someone if you knew who they were. While you remain a name on a piece of paper, you are not a recommendable entity because, in the right minds, you barely even exist.

We often remark that it's a good career move to know all the key people in an industry. And it is. But it is exponentially more valuable to ensure that all the key people know you. This begins to create a snowball effect. It generates that invaluable question, "You know who you should talk to?", to which your name is the answer.

In order to be an expert, you have to be recommended. To be recommended, you have to be a face. Go and meet the key people in your industry. Approach them with good manners, and don't be overbearing, but go out there and get known.

**Key question:**
What is your plan to go from a name on a piece of paper to a living person in the forefront of important players' minds?

## 9. BE CREDIBLE BY ASSOCIATION

Having that logo "Member of the National Chihuahua Caretakers Association" on your biography may be worth its weight in gold. And there are many ways in which you can associate with what I call "credibility enhancers". Start with your industry associations. Many of them will have membership rankings. For example, I'm a member of the Professional Speakers Association and they have an entry-level membership as well as a full membership. Full membership comes with certain benefits.

Some associations will even have courses you can do or requirements you can fulfil to achieve a qualification. In the Professional Speakers Association, you can fulfil certain criteria to become a CSP (Certified Speaking Professional). Achieving this ranking boosts your perceived level of expertise and becomes an additional credential to add to your CV.

It also entails appearing on stage at one of their international conventions, among others who have qualified as CSPs, at a sort of graduation ceremony. This event can be a career-changer because, in one fell swoop, you become a face and a voice to a few thousand key people in your industry.

What is your industry equivalent?

It bears considering that the people in most industry bodies who are best known are the ones who contribute the most. Getting involved and sharing your knowledge, leadership, time or expertise, will get you known, and it's a wonderfully healthy win-win scenario.

Get the membership. Get the credentials. Roll your sleeves up and get your hands dirty, but then think beyond that. What other types of association can enhance your credibility? Could you, for example, have another well-known expert endorse your book, your programme or your event?

When Oprah endorsed books on her show, careers were made. That sort of credibility is worth retirement money. But you can achieve the same effect on a smaller scale. Who else might feature your book, or interview you about your ideas? Perhaps it's time to call them.

Simply appearing on the same lists as celebrities can put you into their bracket in terms of public perception. Being interviewed along with them on a panel will help you to become known as one of them. Appearing on the same agenda does the same.

**Key question:**
Which people or associations could boost your credibility?

## 10. DRESS THE PART

Every industry has a "tone", and your dress code, particularly at public events and in press photographs, will help to determine how people react to you.

I have no intention of being prescriptive, because frankly, that would be counterproductive. You see, the idea of a dress code presents you with an interesting choice: you can either dress in the way that the industry expects (fit in with the group) or you can do something counter-intuitive (stand out as a maverick). Both options have merit, but it's worth approaching your decision with some careful consideration.

If your industry is perceived as sophisticated, corporate, medical or intellectual – in other words, anything fairly "dry" – you might want to wear the suits, the tiny, rimless glasses, the Italian shoes and the conservative haircut.

Or, as scenario planner and author Clem Sunter does, you might want to do the exact opposite. Clem Sunter is known for wearing baggy jerseys and presenting an "absent-minded professor" look when speaking at the highest levels of industry and government all over the world. There is some interesting psychology to this approach. Having been the head of Anglo American, and as a published and respected author, he can get away with a certain quirkiness. In fact, it's even endearing: "He's such a high roller, so very powerful, yet look how friendly he looks, how completely *human*!"

It's worth noting, though, that Clem can "get away" with this sort of dress code *because of* his extensive résumé. For most people starting out in his industry, this image probably wouldn't work at all.

If a 20-something-year-old strategist stepped on to the stage in a baggy jersey, I doubt people would say: "Look how friendly he looks." The likely reaction would be, "That new kid sure isn't taking this very seriously." For a new speaker on the speaking circuit, it would be a lot safer to wear a suit and tie to presentations.

So, what do I recommend for you?

Frankly, it's your choice. Just make sure it's a *considered* choice.

Extremes of physical appearance can also be evocative. Consider Hugh Hefner, *Playboy* owner and founder, who is rarely seen in anything other than a silk dressing gown. You remember him, right? Of course you do. His look is iconic.

Even Stephen Hawking, the British theoretical physicist and author, is instantly recognisable in his high-tech wheelchair. Obviously, this is not a look by design, and we shouldn't be disingenuous, but it remains a fact that he is highly recognisable as the "genius in the wheelchair".

Many experts who work in an arty industry (fashion, design, personal grooming, fine arts, music, photography) will actively cultivate a "gay" persona, even in cases where they are not gay. They're doing it to fit in with the industry and it often works exceptionally well. I am not a big fan of the inauthenticity of this approach, but I lay it on the table for your consideration.

A counter-intuitive approach can also work within the creative spheres. Consider the new breed of rappers and R&B singers who are dressing very smartly on stage – suits and ties, coats and jackets, sometimes even hats and waistcoats – and thus stealing the momentum away from the rather tired, overused *gangsta* look, and effectively becoming thought leaders. They have opted to set themselves apart rather than fit in. Singer Adele was nothing while she dressed like any other British teen, but became a worldwide sensation when she switched to an elegant look.

It's your choice. Consider the tone that you want to convey, and then be consistent with it. Dress for image whenever you're seen in public, whenever you're interviewed and in all of the photos and video footage that you use to promote yourself.

**Key question:**
Is your look distinctive and memorable?

# 11. ACT THE PART

This may sound obvious, but it bears stating: you need to walk the talk.

The body language expert cannot come across as nervous and fidgety. The expert in how to dress beautifully can't afford to look slovenly. You can't lecture others on wealth and drive a pile of smoking rust. (When I launched my CD titled *Is Your Thinking Keeping You Poor?*, I upgraded to a 5-Series BMW.) Your own physicality and behaviour are the strongest representatives of your brand message and they must speak your truth for you.

My wife, who works for a corporate company, recalls the time when a heavily pregnant image consultant gave a talk to her department ... wearing a low-cut top that failed to cover her belly. Needless to say, the delegates all felt uncomfortable, causing the HR department collectively to scratch their heads and wonder why they had hired her. They didn't repeat the mistake.

Does this mean you need to police your actions obsessively? Smile politely at passing nuns? Always be seen holding a fuzzy kitten? Again, it depends on your positioning.

As an example of the antithesis, let's take UK TV-show host, Jeremy Clarkson. The star of a motoring show that is a success story unparalleled in the history of television, *Top Gear*, Jeremy is rather ... rough. That's not to say he's unsophisticated. He's a very intelligent and highly articulate man. But he is also egotistical, a chauvinist, a schoolboy and a rebel, who's constantly having a go at government for their "namby-pamby" policies, and who is seen as being in every way the politically incorrect, spoilt boy-child. And yet – he's one of the best-paid (and loved) entertainers in the world. I am a huge fan of his work.

So no, becoming an expert does not mean that you constantly have to be on your best behaviour. You can be a rough-hewn rebel. But ...

A word of caution. Like all things, the devil-may-care attitude of celebrities can easily be taken too far. You have only to look at the self-destructive behaviour of Britney Spears, Lindsay Lohan, or a plethora of other celebrities, to realise that completely losing the plot can ruin a career. And no, getting out of a car without your panties is not a good publicity move.

That's not what you want to be known for. You are an expert, not a joke. Your goal is to be respected and revered, not loathed or laughed at. Publicity is good, but not at any cost. You are cultivating a reputation as an expert so take your reputation seriously.

Act the part and be the person you portray with integrity. Jeremy Clarkson *really is* the way you see him on TV. *Idols* and *X Factor* judge Simon Cowell *really is* as cynical and straight-talking as he is on his show. Sure, these public figures don't portray themselves as "nice". But there's a certain integrity in who they are and what they do. And over time, we actually come to like them, even respect them, in spite of their rough edges ... sometimes even because of them.

**Key question:**
Does your public persona match the real you?

## 12. LEARN THE NAMES

Names? What names? All of the names in your industry. And all the terminology too.

Here's what tends to happen: you find yourself at an event, networking, socialising and being seen, and someone asks you what you do ...

"I'm a professional cartoonist," you reply.

"Oh, you're a cartoonist! Then you must know old *whatshisname*, right? He draws for the *Obscure Daily*! Don't you just love the way he uses the *whatchacallit* technique?"

You stare back like a deer caught in the headlights. Your interlocutor realises you're just small-fry, a newcomer. Bottom line: it's embarrassing.

You need to know the names of the key players in your industry: the agencies which deal with people who do what you do, the publications which print your kind of content ... and you especially need to know the terminology commonly used in your field.
If you're a little behind on this one, you could:

- subscribe to industry publications
- join interest groups on social media sites liked LinkedIn
- sign up for newsletters and ezines
- go to relevant expos
- read the online bios of the current reigning names
- read the latest books on the topic
- attend industry events and listen to the current experts (always asking The Constant Question(s): What do they do? Why are they seen as experts? What could I do better?)

- treat a reigning expert to a cup of coffee and chat about the basics with them. Ask about the who's who and the daily nitty-gritty of your sphere of interest.

**BOOST YOUR SALES**

It's often important to attend the industry expos so that you know what the latest trends are. This isn't just about keeping up to date – it's actually a valuable sales tool. How will you know what you can offer to your clients if you don't know what's available?

There is a sad dynamic that outdates specialists in their fields. It happens when their techniques start to become dated, but their clientele are too polite to point it out. I can think of at least one person whose business essentially dried up because of his outdated techniques and a reluctance on the part of his customers to point it out. They liked him too much. So they quietly and politely went elsewhere while he held on to the past.

It is not your customers' job to keep you up to date. That is your job.

Your industry, like all others, is constantly evolving, as are the tools of your trade and the techniques available to you. Don't get too comfortable with the old ways. You can become dated and redundant remarkably quickly.

Pay what it takes to get the new equipment. Go to the conventions to keep up. Read the magazines that discuss the trends. Know the terminology and the politics of the day. It may keep you in business for another decade. Because you can offer the latest thing, it may also increase your income.

Fail to know the names – let your knowledge slip behind – and you could go under overnight.

**Key question:**
Do you know who you are and how you are ranked in relation to the key players in your industry?

## 13. DEVELOP A TITLE

A title identifies you to the outside world. It is your point of access: the handle by which the world can get a hold of you.

Your title can be derived from different sources. For instance, it can be your position in your organisation, which gives you instant credibility, provided you are the head of something spectacular. But if you are not the Grand Lofty Marketing Director on High, you can find, generate and create alternative titles.

The marketing folks at Bugatti created the Veyron for one reason and one reason only: to generate for their brand the title of fastest production car in the world. The Veyron is sold at a financial loss. But they have identified that loss as worthwhile simply for the bragging rights. They have crafted a public title on purpose. This is what I call an "est" title: fastest, biggest, smallest, greatest, and so on.

I believe in "est" titles. I believe it's worth your while to do something that is sufficiently splashy and interesting so that the media will pay attention, and journalists can describe you with an "est".

Is there something interesting about what you do that might logically generate a title?

You can even actively go about fashioning a title too. For example, you can be the author of a series of articles on the topic. Or the author of a book. Or the founder of a trust, organisation, or humanitarian cause. You can be a record holder.

Be creative about gathering credentials. For instance, if you need to show leadership know-how, volunteer to be on a governing body ... or get on the board of a Rotary or Toastmasters Club ... or start a leadership brains-trust ... or write a series of articles on leadership.

You can then use your title on business cards, on your website, or even as a footnote on any articles or press releases that you send out. You can use it when you're introduced to speak at an event by supplying it to the person introducing you. If you don't supply it, they won't know what to call you.

A title is a useful way for people to categorise you. And this is a good thing. If they don't know who or what you are, and can't express that who and what to others, then you are not a known entity. If you're not easy to talk about, how will you become known? Develop a title that makes it easy for people to talk about you.

Take care, however, not to overcomplicate your title. I go by the very simple term "professional speaker". My "est" title is "five times SA Public Speaking Champion; no one in Africa has ever won this speaking contest as many times as Douglas".

## QUICK TIP: "OUTTROS"

There is great value in providing your own intro whenever you appear in public. Now start providing an "outtro" as well. This allows you to sell without compromising the purity of your own performance.

"Did you enjoy Joanne's presentation today? Then don't forget to buy her bestselling book afterwards. You can also sign up for her free newsletter, or read more of her articles on her website. Remember, Joanne is the nation's leading sports dietician."

It follows logically that you should develop a title that explains, rather than obscures, what you are. For example, you might refer to yourself as a "kitchen designer". Nice and easy. Clean and simple. I have no interest in calling myself an "empowerment facilitation executive coach consultant". It's not memorable. Not useful. Throw it in the bin and move swiftly along.

**Key question:**
Can you sum up *what you are* in a short phrase?

## 14. USE SIMPLE POSITIONING

This follows from the previous point. Don't be suckered into using long buzzwords and fancy terms. Be the "time management guy" rather than a "facilitator of workplace productivity and process efficiency excellence". Yes, call yourself a "fashion guru" if that's what people understand … an "image consultant" if you're going for a more corporate market … but definitely don't get carried away with nonsense like "personal perception enhancement representative".

Sometimes "The Style Guy" is the better option.

Take the example of New Zealand-based speaker and trainer Robyn Pearce. Robyn specialises in time management. At a time when other time management experts were fiddling around with enormous, self-important monikers, Robyn steadfastly continued to call herself a "time management expert". And guess whose career survived and thrived while her competitors disappeared into a vortex of their own verbiage? You see, when agencies wanted to book someone who dealt with the topic, her name was top of the list because she had been steadfastly punting that one simple idea for years.

Make it crystal clear, memorable and logical. Be that thing. Nothing else.

The same goes for your programme, or what you do. Insecure start-up professionals tend to use big words to make what they do sound important. Experts go straight for the meat of the matter. Take, as another example, the British Channel 4 TV show *Super Size vs Super Skinny*. During series one in 2008, one title featured was "Ban Big Bums!" Doesn't that title just say it all? Is there anything ambiguous about it? Are you in any way unclear about what it might be about? Does it work? Is it memorable?

Exactly!

Professional speaker Justin Cohen has a talk titled, "How to Achieve Great Big Hair-Raising Goals, and Why Most People Don't". Perfectly clear. That will do nicely.

**Key question:**
What is the simplest, most to-the-point title for what you do?

## 15. DEVELOP A STORY OF STRUGGLE

Many of today's how-to books, and almost all inspirational speeches, are based on an individual's struggle story. In a nutshell, this is the tale of how they overcame something. You see, telling people about your success isn't nearly as impactful as telling them about your prior adversity and then your *subsequent* success. The success is interesting. But the pain is *fascinating*. And it's often because people feel that success is bragging, but they can generally relate to the pain.

So don't just tell us about your victories. Tell us about your darkest hour. Tell us about the most painful moments.

Observe the difference between these two introductions:

A: "This is Gary. He's the author of *Think More Cleverly* and he will be talking to us about how to use the power of strategic thinking to improve our lives ..."

Not bad. But this is better:

B: "This is Gary. He came from an impoverished background, and had to borrow textbooks during his school years. But Gary discovered the power of strategic thinking early on and used it to rise from obscurity and become the head of a multinational corporation. He is now the author of *Think More Cleverly* and today he will be talking to us about how to use the power of strategic thinking to improve your life, just like he did in his own ..."

If possible, develop one of your own because a struggle story adds legitimacy to your message. And it shouldn't just be a part of your introduction. You can use it constantly in your messages as well.

You may have frowned at the sentence "... develop one of your own". No, this doesn't mean that you should bend the truth and fabricate a story. But it does mean that you should take your own story and hone the way in which you tell it, write it and present it. In other words, choose the interesting and relevant parts and position it for audience consumption.

Also, your struggle story doesn't actually have to be as dramatic as the rags to riches example above. It could be smaller than that, quirkier, even humorous. Here's an example of a very simple struggle story:

"Bobby is here this morning to coach us in the use of humour in corporate presentations. Bobby admits that humour didn't come naturally to him at first. He had to learn the principles the hard way. In fact, he fondly recalls his first attempt at stand-up comedy in a nightclub, which he later described to three separate therapists as the longest two hours he'd ever experienced in a ten-minute period ... But Bobby didn't care. He wiped off the tomato residue and persisted! He was determined to learn the principles of humour, and today, he is acknowledged as an expert in the field. Moreover, these days, he is hardly ever pelted with fruit."

You don't need to have survived cancer, been eaten by a shark or have climbed Mount Everest to have a good story. You just need to show that you overcame a difficult situation and so can help others to do the same. This is the nature of a struggle story.

If you are completely stumped for your own struggle story, bend this idea slightly and talk about how you have already taught others to overcome their problems with your expertise. By doing so, you essentially adopt the struggle story of others.

Let's take a moment to focus on the importance of pain in the struggle story. I've found that when training others in presentation skills, it is exponentially more effective to start by speaking about my own public speaking disasters. Not only are they interesting (and in many cases, hilarious), but they help the audience to relate. When I then go on to provide solutions to the problems I've described, I have their emotional buy-in. As teaching tools go, the pain that precedes the victory is an especially powerful one.

**Key question:**
What have you overcome in order to be what you are?

# 16. FIND A WAY TO BE THE MOST OR THE GREATEST

... like the makers of the Bugatti Veyron.

Clearly, this is not something that you can do early on in your career. It requires that you establish yourself and become proficient in what you do, and then do a little more – or, indeed, a great deal more – in order to stand out.

As you develop and start to become significant in your industry, look for ways to develop a point of distinction, a unique selling proposition. This is something that differentiates you from the crowd, something that makes you "more", and more "wow". You might be *the most booked* or *the most published* or *the only one in your industry ever to ...* or *the only one in your industry who hasn't ...* The more spectacular, the better.

My own unique selling proposition, as mentioned before, is to have been the only South African ever to have won the Southern African Public Speaking Championships, through Toastmasters, a record five times. My goal is ultimately to win the World Championships, which would then position me among a group of people who can quite literally call themselves the best in the world. That would be quite the point of distinction! But for now, my current positioning works well for me. It creates a perception of competence and excellence and differentiates me from other speakers.

There are many ways to manufacture unique positioning. For instance, if you were a personal fitness guru, you could organise a unique event, such as having one hundred strong men lifting a truck off the ground. If you were smart about it, you might then build in a message about proper lifting techniques, and how not to hurt your back, so that the whole thing could be viewed as an educational and awareness-building event. Thereafter, you would be the fitness guru who organised the hundred-man truck lift (as seen on TV!).

Or if you were a chef, you could stage a publicity event in which you prepared the world's largest pizza, or the world's longest chain of interlinked doughnuts, and thereby get yourself into the *Guinness Book of World Records*. Afterwards you could donate the pizza to an orphanage ... you get the idea.

Make it spectacular, media-worthy and memorable. Also, make it relevant because you may be remembered for it for a long time.

**Key question:**
How much greater could you be if you *really* tried?

## 17. DEVELOP A FREE EDUCATIONAL GUIDE

Let's say that you are a professional wedding photographer. You know that you have to be a face and a voice, so you've decided to exhibit at a bridal expo (certainly not the only public forum, but sometimes a good one).

Your work may be the very best on display, but you can do more to position yourself as the stand-out leader of the pack.

You can develop and give away free educational materials. You might detail useful topics such as "10 things for a bride to remember on her wedding day" or "5 ways to get the most out of your photos".

If you are clever, you will play on fears as well, *a la* "4 things that typically go wrong at weddings, and how to avoid them". Do you think that a bride might want to have that information? Of course she would! And you are the expert who has solved her problem and helped her to avoid pain during the most important event of her life. This is true thought leadership.

It constitutes the ultimate in mutually beneficial relationships, showing your target market that you are not just an operator, but you are actually on their side in this process. You are an advocate and a trusted aide.

The essence of this arrangement is that you are giving value upfront. You give first in the belief that they will reward you with their business later on.

It makes you an authority and a generous guide. Plus, it's easy to do.

If you don't have the ideas yourself, speak to your clients. Tell them openly that you're developing a free educational giveaway and would like their help. What have they learnt that might be useful?

What tips would they be happy to pass on to you? What do they fear or worry about? Pain and fear are often excellent generators of thought-leadership content.

The very process of carrying out this exercise is an opportunity to impress in and of itself. It's both a display of humility and caring, and an act of professionalism.

Over the years, as the information continues to come to you, based on your practice of the ask The Constant Question principle, ensure that you continually update your educational handouts.

And remember, every update is an excuse for publicity. Be smart about it too. If you keep an eye on trends and events, you can always spot opportunities to re-engineer your educational materials to fit new circumstances and new needs. Constant adaptation will keep you at the forefront of your industry.

**DON'T FORGET TO BE INTERESTING**

I once used the services of a tax consultant. He sent out a monthly email newsletter, which contained great content, but which I rarely found myself reading. The problem was the title. It was boring and didn't pique my interest in any way.

If you are going to send out a monthly newsletter, make sure that the title shows some clear value to the reader. As a simple example, use "4 Ways to Pay Less" rather than "Monthly Tax Newsletter".

Also, can you add an interesting visual to your handout? Does it look like the sort of thing that might be kept and pinned up at home?

**Key question:**
What sort of handout would your target market truly appreciate?

# 18. HOARD AND PUBLICISE PRAISE

Do you have testimonials from clients, customers, peers or notorieties? If so, use them. If not, start to collect them. They are hugely valuable to you, and should be displayed prominently on walls and websites, products and pamphlets, stands, displays and guides.

And if you are absolutely stumped, think about people you may have worked with, spoken in front of, met or mentored in the past. Would they be willing to scribble two lines about how knowledgeable you are on the topic, how reliable you are, how much they liked your winning smile?

There's also a big trend towards video testimonials that can be featured on websites and incorporated into presentations. A few lines of text with a name can be very powerful. But a video clip of the CEO talking about your wonders and virtues is even better. They can also be sent out on social media and incorporated into your website as publicity and credibility builders.

One of the great things about video testimonials is that they are often easier to acquire than written ones. Instead of having to sit and pen thoughts, your prospect simply reacts to your request, "May I film you saying that?" It can be done instantly with little effort on their part.

**LIGHT-BULB MOMENT**

Here's an additional idea: when you are asked to do anything for free, consider agreeing to it, but request a testimonial in return. Professionals are always approached to do things for free. Quid pro quo.

Always remember that the best time to ask for a testimonial is when your client is raving about you. Leaving it for a couple of days after the fact may allow the fires to cool. While you are receiving praise, ask whether they might be willing to put it in writing or appear in a video clip. If they are gushing, capture the gush. Gush is valuable. Gush builds credibility.

**Key question:**
What more could you do to generate references and referrals?

## 19. SPEAK THE LANGUAGE OF RESULTS

Most people – indeed, most *companies* – involved in the process of selling anything, tend to sell the wrong thing. In spite of countless books, courses and articles advising otherwise, they still sell the features and not the results.

As an expert, it's important that you get your mind around this one early on and truly learn to sell outcomes. Outcomes, outcomes, outcomes! This is your new mantra because outcomes are everything. Outcomes are what they care about at the high levels where money-based decisions are made. Outcomes are what build reputations. If you think and speak in the language of outcomes, it will change how you go about your marketing, and can dramatically alter your success rate in bringing in new business.

Here, then, is the test: does the bulk of your marketing material focus on the *delivery mechanism*? Or does it focus on how what you do, or what you sell, changes the end-state of your customer? Your marketing material should all be about the end-state of your customer.

In the simplest terms: you do not sell an exercise machine. You sell six-pack abs and a beach-ready body. The exercise machine is merely the mechanism for delivery.

Let's start with your website. Do this test today: does the bulk of the wording describe *how* you do what you do? Or does it focus on what will be different in the life of the customer after you have done it? In other words, is it about you, or is it about the results for them?

It's the difference between *Douglas teaches presentation skills* versus *Douglas helps you to win your pitches and lead more effectively from the front of the room.*

Now scour your other marketing materials, brochures and guides. Are you speaking the language of results? How about during your pitches to clients? Do you start with a half-hour dissertation on the history of your business? Or do you go straight for the jugular with results-oriented language?

I will argue that as an expert, most of your clients will be high level. For this reason, they are generally not the people who will actually be using your product or service personally; that honour tends to go to lower-level functionaries. As an expert, your clients will tend to be big-picture people. And they don't care how it works; they care about what it does for them, their business, their career, their future. They care about results.

Now, here is the good news: when you get results for high-level people, they will talk to other high-level people. Results generate the question, "You know who you should talk to?", with *you* as the answer. This is why results are so important.

Results are also important because they raise your value. If you "do a thing", you are a commodity. And a commodity can be replaced with another commodity. But if you "get a result", you are valuable. This distinction changes your pay scale.

At a later stage, we will discuss how your fee increases in proportion to the severity of the problem you solve, and how charging for results allows you to be more expensive than someone who charges for "deeds done".

Getting results counts in a big way towards building your profile as an expert as well. Take the example of a consultant. Rather than just talking about her credentials, she could cite the companies which have experienced great results because of her intervention. That's what high-level buyers really care about.

Good idea: Sonja has spoken for companies like BMW and IBM.

Great idea: Sonja increased efficiency at BMW and IBM by 10%! The CEO raved about her results, and said that every large multinational should hire her and learn the lessons she has to share. He gave her a free car and an island and said she totally rocked!

When people and organisations you have trained or worked with report your excellent results, your credibility is increased. Again, though, don't forget to ask for the testimonials as most companies that you work for will simply not bother. Remember, building your career is your problem, not theirs.

**LIGHT-BULB MOMENT**

If you need the credentials, how about taking the initiative to consult for a company for free in exchange for a free testimonial and the ability to use them as a reference if you succeed? Not only is this a good way to build credibility, but it's also a great way to sell into that company again later on. "Hey, she was great last time! Let's get her again." One word of caution, though: free work has an expiry date. You can only do it in the early stages of building your professional career. Do it once you're up and running, and you will be seen as cheap.

**Key question:**
What could you set up this week that would translate directly into results?

## 20. GATHER PAYING CLIENTS

Professionals often question whether or not to work for free. And while I believe that there is value in doing so initially, I want to caution you not to continue doing it over time. Do not! This is, after all, your chosen profession and, presumably, your means of income. Not only do you need the cash, but *not* getting paid is detrimental to your perception as a professional. Your premium level fee, and the perceived value of what you do, is a very big part of the total perception of your quality.

Experts are not cheap.

Interestingly, the more expensive you are, the better you are perceived to be. Illogical, but true. Welcome to the game of perceptions!

And while you don't want to price yourself out of the market (and you do want to ensure your clients feel they are getting their money's worth), undercharging actually hurts you. It devalues you and causes you to be thought of as "junior".

Another interesting off-spin of undercharging is that it will probably bring in lots of piecemeal work. And this is a bad thing. Honestly, you don't want a diary full of time-consuming, low profit-margin work. If you are doing lots of work for small profit margins, you will exhaust yourself and never become wealthy. If, alternatively, you are doing much less work for much higher profit margins, you will conserve your own energy, be more focused and earn more.

Moreover, here is a thought to chew on: if you spend a great deal of time working for low-paying clients – listen carefully – *they will become your norm.* You will begin to see them as your reality, and it will change your professional behaviour. You will act in ways commensurate with low-level operatives in your industry. This won't do. It is the wrong momentum for you.

So, as you go about positioning yourself as an expert in your industry, you don't need to be the most expensive ... but you certainly can't afford to be the cheapest.

You should also occasionally jettison the low-end of your business to clear up your diary, and your focus, for higher-level clientele. Don't keep low-paying clients just because they have always been around.

Value yourself, and others will do the same. Display your sense of your own value through your fee.

**WHAT IF THEY CAN'T MEET MY FEE?**

Aha! Here is a simple solution. Ask your potential client whether they would like to trade equal value, rather than pay a cash amount. Let's say that you are selling to or consulting for a company that makes car tyres. They could supply you with an equivalent value in tyres as barter for your services. That's fair enough, and it's a great way to keep working and get value in return for your expertise, even when clients can't actually afford you.

And there are other clever ways around this problem. For instance, you might give a slight discount in return for multiple sales. Or recommendations for further business with their contacts.

But don't ever simply discount your price with no give and take from the client. Why should you? If they are asking for a cheaper price, they need to provide you with equivalent value in some shape or form. When last did you walk into a store, buy a can of Coke, and successfully convince the store manager that you only had two-thirds of the sticker price?

Why should your business operate any differently?

**Key question:**
Do you know what fees the top players in your industry currently demand?

## 21. BE DECLARATIVE AND STATE WHAT YOU ARE AN EXPERT IN

Here is an interesting balancing act: to truly qualify as an expert, which is a publically created perception, you have to be called an expert by others. Not yourself.

That said, unless you announce yourself to the world, they may never get around to calling you an expert.

The good news is that announcing your expertise doesn't have to be a cringeworthy, bragging-at-cocktail parties sort of affair.

You simply build the wording into introductions and bylines. For instance, when you are publically introduced at a speaking engagement, your introduction could say, "Mike is an expert on bodybuilding techniques. He's spent years studying the craft, learning from the masters, and applying his knowledge in his own workouts. He has been through it all, from the struggle to gain mass, to painful injury and back again. He understands the challenges that bodybuilders face, and has worked with many top athletes in helping them to prepare for competitions. Please help me to welcome Mike."

When Mike writes for industry publications, the attribution at the end could also read, "Mike Strongarm is a twenty-year veteran of the gym. You name it, this bodybuilding expert has lifted it! Visit Mike's website at ..."

Notice that in the above scenario about a speaking engagement, Mike has provided his own intro. You should do this too. There is nothing wrong with stating publically that you know your stuff, and it sounds highly credible coming from an MC or chairperson, who introduces you at an event.

If you do speak publically on your area of expertise (and I will encourage you to do so and explain the importance in another chapter), beware of an interesting dynamic that will come into play: people often don't know how to read intros. They will typically say cringeworthy things like "Mike asked me to read out his list of achievements."

This is actually worse than if you'd had no introduction at all. It sounds conceited and staged. So, while it may sound ridiculous to specify, when you hand an intro to an MC, ask them not to say, "Mike said to read this ..." They should just read it.

**QUICK TIP**

Being an expert is not just about knowledge. It's also about personality. And you can begin showing your personality in an intro. Why not build in some humanity? Perhaps a little humour?

**Key question:**
Have you developed an introduction for others to use?

## 22. DEVELOP PRODUCTS

Dear Aspiring Industry Expert: have you written that book yet?

Each time we reach December, you probably think to yourself: *I wish I had written my book this year. If I had, next year might be different. I would be more prosperous; I'd have more clients approaching me; my life would be lived on a grander scale. Groupies would congregate and throw undergarments.*

And your suppositions are correct. So, will you let another December flit by without it? In a bigger sense, do you have sufficient years left in your career trajectory to sustain *not* writing it this year?

In my book, *50 Ways to Become a Better Speaker*, I included a chapter on how to become a professional speaker on your local circuit. It referred to a true story about a time when I was just getting into the industry, and asked my agent what I could do to boost my own speaking career. The question I posed was "What is the number one thing speakers can do to get ahead?"

My agent explained that the same principle applied in any industry. To quote her exact words, "When you have written a book, people regard you as one step down from God."

Nothing increases your credibility or visibility quite like having a book in print. And it's not critical that your book should be a Dostoyevskian masterpiece and a *New York Times* bestseller. It's the simple fact of the thing that counts. People take you more seriously when you've been published. You are regarded as an authority.

Of course, I'd like to encourage you to write a *really good* book, rather than just churning out rubbish. Being the author of a genuine bestseller, or of the definitive title on a topic, certainly won't hurt your reputation. Plus, why would you want to put your name to something slapdash?

The second and obvious advantage to publishing a book is that you can use it to gain publicity. There's the launch, the media coverage, the potential for interviews on radio and television and more. In fact, it's even conceivable that the people who find and buy your book in the bookstores may hire you to do what you write about, turning your book into a sales tool too. It even helps in business meetings with potential clients. Handing over a free copy of your book is impressive. You have clearly been involved in this industry for a while, and you obviously know your stuff.

And the third advantage is that it becomes a part of your title …

"This is Joanne. She is the author of *Sound Principles for Cooking Overweight Guppies*."

This carries considerable weight.

Some speakers' agents urge their clients to consider self-publishing instead of submitting their manuscript to a publisher. Their rationale is that you can potentially make more money by selling your own books at events than by having them on the shelves in bookstores where your profit is significantly less.

The counter-argument is that a publisher can achieve greater reach for you by retailing your books and you will gain more publicity. And there is an element of authenticity and satisfaction to having your book accepted by a publisher rather than simply paying for its publication yourself.

It's your choice, although I would tend to recommend commercial publishing with a big house much more strongly. Either way, writing a book is certainly a worthy investment of your time.

I have noticed that people are strangely hesitant to get started with the project of book-writing. In 2006, immediately after I had published my first book, a fellow professional speaker told me adamantly that he now wanted to do the same! He's been saying the same thing, adamantly, for the past seven years now.

Conversely, a friend of mine confided in me last year that he wanted to write a book. Earlier this year, his finished manuscript was accepted by a publisher. That's how it's done.

You will not become an industry expert by talking about it. You will become an industry expert by doing it. Be a doer.

That covers the idea of writing a book. But a book is not your only product option.

Another idea is to develop programmes, such as audio and video products. This is usually perceived as being easier to do than writing a book, and it's certainly quicker. It may not rank on the same level as writing a book in the world of public perceptions, but it's certainly an excellent idea. I currently have three audio CDs and a video DVD on offer. Why have multiple products? Because if your followership likes what you do, they will buy as much as you will offer.

There are two ways in which you can go about recording a programme, be it audio or video. You can either do the recording in private, talking into a microphone or camera (usually from a script) or you can record a talk or training session you do live, and turn that into a CD or DVD.

Many experts choose to do a combination of the two. They may, for example, produce an audio CD that goes like this:

(Studio voice-over): "Hi, my name is Joanne. Thanks for buying my course on social skills. I'd like to start by sharing with you some tips on how to overcome social anxiety. Listen to what I told this audience ..."

(Cuts to public presentation, recorded live): "There are five ways to overcome social anxiety ..." And so on.

So, which should you do first: a book or CD?

CDs and DVDs are quicker. So if you're in a rush to get a product out and start building credibility, you could start by recording two or three audio CDs and a video, and begin to market yourself with these, while writing a book in the background.

Personally, I did it the other way around, and started with the book. But the choice is yours – just be sure to become a producer of materials soon. And don't stop at your first product. A book is good, but in isolation, it's not enough. Do the CD as well. Then do the second book. And the second CD. Keep going, and as the total weight of your output grows, so will your reputation.

At this point, I've only mentioned books, CDs and DVDs. There are many, many more channels. Here is a list of options for products and means of expressing your expertise that you can develop to increase your total professional presence:

- Books
- DVDs

- DVD sets
- CDs
- CD sets
- Audio books
- Series of online blogs
- Speeches
- Workshops
- Seminars and bootcamps
- Workbooks
- Teleseminars
- Posters
- Branded mugs
- E-courses
- Newsletters
- PDF guides
- Downloadable MP3 guides
- And so on, limited only by your energy and imagination.

**BOOST YOUR SALES**

If people like what you do, they will generally want more. Experts tend to develop tribes, who will happily buy anything that they offer. Sometimes, they will even tell you that they are waiting for the next thing, and ask when you will produce it. So keep on producing.

Also, find ways to remove barriers to purchase. People will generally buy your products if you make it easy for them to do so. If they are not available to peruse, people won't buy them. If you can't accept their method of payment, they won't buy either. If you don't have change, they won't buy. If they can't click on a simple link on your website to purchase your products ... Well, you get the picture.

Developing products, and especially books, is a very big deal. I can't force you into your writing room or recording studio, and I can do no more than urge you to sit in that chair and tell you that it matters. But let me ask you: will another December arrive and catch you bookless? Or will you take the initiative and radically change your place in your industry? Will you keep telling people that you mean to do it? For the next seven years? Or will you simply sit down and begin?

**Key question:**
What sort of book, relating to your industry, would *you* buy and read?

## 23. OFFER YOUR EXPERTISE TO THE MEDIA

Media channels are your friends. They are your means of duplicating, replicating and multiplying yourself, your voice and your message of thought leadership. Print, radio and TV. Learn to love them. Learn to use them. They are actually much more accessible than you may imagine.

For newcomers, the idea of getting on to TV, or having an article published in a newspaper, may seem daunting, if not an utter impossibility. But it's actually not that difficult.

Print articles in newspapers and magazines are probably my single most valuable form of advertising, and I write a lot of articles. In fact, I keep a running log of media submissions for each year, tracking which media outlets I have sent articles and submissions to.

I use the basic principles of public relations: give value to the publication and, in return, they will publicise your details. What is value? Value is generally the useful, educational insights that you can provide by merit of your knowledge. If you were an expert at audio sound systems, for example, you could write an article on the best way to set up sound systems for a concert. You could also include a quick summary of the top five mistakes that amateurs make when doing so and how those mistakes impact negatively on the concert.

This information would be useful to anyone setting up a concert, and if they happen to be your target market, you are writing something of value to them. If you can prove to an editor that this is the case, then you are very likely to be published. The pay-off is that your target market will read your article, and take note that you know how to set up audio systems for concerts. The next logical step is for them to call you and book your services.

The more publications you are featured in, the greater your total presence.

I write regular articles for a number of local publications, and I've even written for international ones. My experience is that editors aren't usually very good at responding to queries, but they are generally willing to publish a good, completed article that fits in with the tone of their publication. On a couple of occasions, I've written to editors and received no response. Then I've tried sending an article, and in a few days' time, I've seen the article appear in print. A great many editors seem to be oddly reclusive, but if you provide value, they can become a big part of your expert positioning efforts.

Getting on to a radio talk show is usually a matter of going on to the station's website and having a look at the formats for the different shows. Select one that best suits what you want to talk about, and contact the producer or presenter of that particular show. State your idea for an interview feature in a succinct but punchy and interesting way, and leave a number of contact options for them to reach you with. The same principle applies to television.

Here is an example of a catchy and interesting email to the producer of a show:

Dear Mr Flynn

Congratulations on producing an excellent show!

My name is Stan Boxoffice, and I have a topic that I believe would interest your listeners.

As a three-times winner of the National Photographic Contest, I have seen some incredible things over the past year, most of which ordinary people would never get to see. I've been trapped at the bottom of an abandoned mine; I've travelled through the desert in a donkey cart; and I've even been surrounded by rioting vegetarians with nothing more than a two-day old hot dog with which to defend myself. I would love to share these stories with your listeners, and to offer some useful, practical tips to anyone who shares my interest in photography.

> This would be a good time to do such an interview as next month is International Photography Month.
>
> Please don't hesitate to contact me should you need any further information, and thank you for your time.
>
> Kind Regards
> Stan Boxoffice
>
> (Telephone number)
> (Cellphone number)
> (Email address)
> (Website)
> (Courier pigeon)
> (Cave)

Each of the various media outlets presents you with opportunities to become more visible. If you offer them quality content, they are more likely to develop trust in you and use your insights repeatedly. There are a number of editors and producers who now approach me at regular intervals, and this is greatly valuable to my business.

And repetition is the name of the game when it comes to publicising yourself in this way. One article is good. But five consecutive articles will be ten times better.

And once you have been published or featured in one media outlet, use the momentum to get into another. If you've been in *Fortune*, it will be easier to get into *Forbes*. But suggest it to them; don't wait for them to find you.

**THE BIG ONE**

It is worth noting that television is still number one in terms of publicity. You cannot beat its reach and impact. I highly recommend writing articles and using social media, and these are powerful tools, but they do not even begin to approach the power of The Box.

Most of the truly big names in any industry are known by virtue of their TV shows. As an example, think of the Kardashians. To the utter bewilderment of people with intelligence everywhere, the Kardashians have become more than just a brand; they are more akin to an empire.

And although a great number of people read about them in the tabloids and follow them in the social media, it has to be said that they would not do so had the Ks not appeared on television first.

Oprah used to generate insta-celebrity with her show, particularly for authors of books.

Television is powerful. In the media world, nothing beats having your own TV show, or appearing regularly on someone else's. Having said that, it is also the single hardest medium to break into. Social media is growing and thriving as a marketing outlet specifically because anyone can get into it. TV is tough. But if you can crack it, nothing is more effective.

**GET NOTICED BY BEING INTERESTING**

If you are submitting to a magazine or newspaper, be sure to attach a high-resolution picture of yourself, as well as your title and contact details. Also, use a catchy and interesting title. Sure, you can pen a piece titled, "How to add the element of surprise to your writing", but it's not nearly as emotive as "Give your readers a serious wedgie!"

And everybody is using safe, nice titles. If you do it too, you won't stand out. A little colour, a little controversy, can make you very memorable. Why not "How to Kill the Pope"?

Be interesting, and it will help you to get noticed. Be consistently interesting, and in time media outlets will come to rely on you. He has edge, they'll say. She has pizazz. And the more edge and the more pizazz you present over time, the greater your visibility will become. Also, when submitting anything for consideration, ask yourself, "What is the story here?" And most importantly, "Where is the value?"

**BECOME A REGULAR**

Have you noticed how talk-show hosts, on both radio and TV, repeatedly use the same experts? They do this because those experts made themselves known and available to the producers of that show, and then provided consistent value. That's how Dr Phil started, by appearing on "Oprah" as a specialist in his field.

Think about this one from the point of view of the show's producers. They don't want the bother of repeatedly sourcing different experts to comment on the same topic. If you are the person they know, and you give them good, quality thoughts and opinions, they will use and re-use your expertise.

Once you become a known entity, you can begin to take on somewhat of a director's role: propose what topics and angles should be covered next. The easier you make their job, the more likely it is that they'll continue to use your services.

You can even encourage them to use you more frequently by proactively offering suggestions that drive their content.

Picture this scenario: you're an expert on writing. You've sourced and then featured on a radio talk show in an interview about "How to Plot a Compelling Novel". Once the interview is done, you point out that there is a nationwide fiction-writing contest coming up next month. You then offer a second interview, this time on the topic of "How to Enter Writing Contests".

Of course, after that, you could point out that plotting a novel, as you discussed in the first interview, is only the first step.

"Why don't you let me do a weekly series of features on how to go about writing and publishing a book, from one end to the other? We could move from plotting to characterisation to research techniques to scene-setting ... "

**Key question:**
Which shows could you appear on to discuss issues, and what additional issues could you cover for greater mileage?

## 24. USE SOCIAL MEDIA

Are you on Facebook yet? Myspace? LinkedIn? Twitter? YouTube? Google Plus?

If not, you need to be. These forums are free, and they will increase your presence considerably. They may or may not create new business for you, but they will increase your total presence and "findability" factor, which could lead to new business. Moreover, they will keep you front-of-mind with your existing clients, which can lead to repeat business.

Online presence is very important and some professionals use it as their sole means of reaching out to target audiences.

Of course, as with all marketing channels, there are better and worse ways to use these tools.

Over the past few years, as these media have become popular, a couple of guidelines have emerged, which you can use as rules of thumb.

The first is that you need to have a website. If people read your tweets and want to know more about you, the exercise will have been in vain if there is no logical channel for them to follow. Conversely, they should also be able to sign up to follow you on social media from your website.

The next rule is never to use any of these media to do hard-core marketing. It is considered much more effective to be at least slightly interesting or entertaining, and *then* to have a subtle marketing message alongside your comments.

Take Facebook, for example. Most users will simply write little snippets about what they are doing at any given time, often with a humorous or amusing slant. They may post quick quotes or snippet-style ideas. You can do the same, and then from time to time, you could announce a new product, book, idea, article or video clip.

The idea is to let people get to know the real you, not to bombard them with advertisements. It creates a sense of intimacy between you and the key players in your industry, as well as potential clients. You'd be amazed at how interested other people will be in what you do every day, and your thoughts and opinions on various matters.

Twitter is slightly different to Facebook. Although many people use Facebook and Twitter in the same manner, there is a subtle difference. Facebook tends to be more about what you're doing, while Twitter is generally used for thoughts, observations and announcements that may be of value to others.

LinkedIn is slightly different once again, and this one is absolutely essential for you. LinkedIn is a business site that works in essentially the same way as Facebook, just not in a social way. It is a purely business-oriented platform. You can update your status, but not to say, "OMG! My puppy just lost a milk tooth! Cutie-poo! Lol!" LinkedIn is for announcements such as, "I've just uploaded a new article to my site. Read about The 6 Skills That Make or Break Your Business here …"

Also, one of the great merits of LinkedIn is the ability to join groups. As a professional speaker, I join just about every group that has to do with conferences, marketing, professional speaking, sales, business networking and events that I can find. I then post regular articles and comments in these groups so that I am visible to all the right people.

I personally tend to send the same content to both Facebook and Twitter, including a bit of personal matter and a bit of business advice. However, my LinkedIn posts are purely business.

Aside from LinkedIn, it's a good idea to look at social media as a PR tool rather than a marketing tool. The main principle in PR is to give value constantly and thereafter, to include a subtle marketing message. Giving value on social media sites may mean providing free articles, quotes, tips, insights or entertaining video footage. It's up to you what you load on to these pages, but bear in mind that everything you upload communicates something about your brand.

That brings us to our next rule of thumb: be very, very careful about uploading anything too contentious, unless your brand image is specifically about being contentious. You may want to avoid hard-core political views, sexual commentary, foul language and the like. Also, don't gossip or backbite online. Don't participate in fights. Don't show racism or bigotry. It will come back to haunt you.

These things can come back to bite you in the fleshy, padded area in your professional life so never lose sight of the fact that even though this type of forum is casual, it is still creating an impression of you in the minds of potential clients.

A good idea is to have a link to such forums from your website: "Follow Joe the Sexy Mechanic on Twitter by clicking here". This allows people who are interested in you, and in what you do, to become "friends" of yours online.

If you find it too time-consuming to log in to each of these social media sites and update your status on each site in turn, you may want to use a free download program such as Tweetdeck or Hootsuite. These programs are free to download and can easily be found with a Google search. They allow you to type your thoughts just once and then have them distributed to all your social media sites in one go. You can either do this from your computer, or, as I generally do, from your phone, as you go about your business during the day.

Here is an example of the kind of content I post on Twitter. I have simply gathered my last few posts, over a day-and-a-half period, as a quick cross-section:

> Tonight I'll be doing an educational session on contest speeches at a TM club in Pretoria.
>
> Great Toastmasters meeting in Pretoria tonight. Enjoyed presenting the educational. Going to listen to my audible book on the drive home.
>
> If you don't get time to read, I recommend http://Audible.com. I'm working my way through a Grisham novel and a Kiyosaki financial book.
>
> Today we started the process of editing my book, *Own Your Industry*, with Penguin. :-)
>
> Preparing my content for the third in a series of radio interviews tomorrow. Topic: Speak like a thought leader.
>
> Interview done: How to Handle High Consequence Presentations Like a Thought Leader will air in the UK on Monday. Will provide the link soon.
>
> Having fun taking loooong photos with the panoramic function on iPhone. Bring me a wide person!
>
> #OwnYourIndustry: Are you constantly writing for your industry? You can't be a thought leader unless you're producing thought that leads.
>
> New Top Gear tonight! :-)

**RED LIGHT!**

A word of caution: beware of the built-in time-wasters on these sites. Facebook, for example, has a function where you can get involved in "virtual farming". While it's lots of fun, it also takes up a lot of your time. Remember, you are an expert, not a computer game addict. This is a tool, not a toy.

**Key question:**
Whose online updates do you personally follow because they are genuinely interesting?

## 25. ACQUIRE THIRD-PARTY ENDORSEMENTS

It's useful to have others promote you as an expert. On a practical note, here is a question for you: who is promoting you, and why should they?

I would like you to start arming your enablers by design.

A best-case scenario is when people love what you do to such an extent that they sell you to others simply because they want to. This implies that you do your job so proficiently that you not only satisfy your clients, but absolutely delight them. Naturally, that should always be your goal. Go above and beyond, and offer exceptional value whenever you work for someone.

But there are other ways you can actively cultivate third-party endorsements too. You could offer a commission to anyone who recommends you for an assignment. Or you may even ask happy clients if they can recommend anyone else who would benefit from what you do.

Or, as I mentioned earlier, you could cultivate a relationship with the editor of the trade magazine, and ask that she think of you when they get enquiries for experts.

**BOOST YOUR SALES**

Do key people have samples of your products? Did you send the editor of your industry magazine a sample of your book? Does your events coordinator have your CD and DVD? Do you arm your enablers with tangible sales tools for your cause?

I like to go so far as to give framed copies of my articles in *Forbes* or *Entrepreneur Magazine* to my speaking agents. My hope is that they go up in the office, displaying me to their customers and keeping me front-of-mind among those who are best positioned to elevate my brand.

**Key question:**
How many third parties are on your list to approach regarding endorsement, and how do you plan to impress them?

## 26. DEVELOP PARTNERSHIPS AND SPONSORSHIPS

Some professionals find great value in this concept. Others have little luck with it. Essentially, the idea is to approach a corporate company with a big wallet (and a similar ethos to your own) and to offer an opportunity for publicity in return for funding your projects.
The key is to find a logical fit, and to offer the company undeniable value.

For example, let's say that you are an expert stunt car driver. You might approach Subaru to sponsor you, provide you with a car, and pay your salary as you film your new documentary series: "Hooligans of the Highways – becoming a real stunt driver".

Subaru would then put their branding on your car, outfit, and so on, and you would spend a little time on your programme discussing the merits of their car. You'd do it in a way that is natural and without sounding like an infomercial ("But wait! There's more!").

It's often not as hard as you may think to get in front of the right people to make a pitch for sponsorship. You need to approach either the marketing manager, or the CEO (or both). You also need to speak the right language. Tell them you have a potential branding and sponsorship opportunity that's worth a lot of money for their brand. Ask for 20 minutes of their time to run the idea by them on a no-obligation basis. Remember, you need to speak the language of outcomes; these are big-picture people.

If you get your meeting (as is the case with all successful sales pitches), you don't want to spend too much time telling your potential sponsor how brilliant you are. You need only convince them that you are an expert. Quickly. Then, more importantly, you should show an understanding of their business, their target market, their clients and their needs. Once you've done this, all that's left is to help them by displaying their logo and products prominently and proudly.

You could also go for what is called a "soft dollars" arrangement. This is the same basic principle, but instead of being paid money, you receive equivalent value. For instance, you could partner with a radio station and allow them to put their banners up at your event. Then they might give you a certain amount of free advertising through their channel.

What might sponsors pay for, wholly or in part?

- The cost of publishing your books
- The cost of producing your CDs or DVDs
- Your equipment (such as the car and driving gear in the Subaru example)
- A series of speaking tours
- Your venue
- Items or gifts that you give away
- Shirts or promotional materials
- Travelling costs
- Team events
- Infrastructure for world record breaking attempts
- Competition efforts (think of Red Bull sponsoring certain X-games and certain participants).

**Key question:**
Which organisations have similar goals to yours and might consider a partnership?

# 27. ADD YOUR UNIQUE SIGNATURE TO YOUR WORK

In your early days in an industry, you tend to do what you're told in the way you are told to do it. This qualifies you for the less-than-flattering Working Drone status described earlier.

As you become more proficient, you begin bringing your unique personality to the mix, and as you attain expert status, you begin consciously adding your own unique signature to your work.

I like to state it this way: beyond excellence lies customisation.

Think of it: all practitioners who take their craft seriously will eventually arrive at a sort of standardised level of excellence. This is the level at which you are just as good as anyone else who is excellent at what you do. To go beyond this point – to break through the "mere excellence" barrier – you must add your own personal flourish to your work. Beyond excellence lies customisation.

I once met an architect whose unique signature is the addition of roof gardens to his homes and commercial buildings. He loves them, specialises in them, and recommends them to his clients, who are generally so impressed with his past work that they allow him to add roof gardens to their projects. He has become known – and widely requested – as a direct result of the unique signature he has added to his work. He is the roof garden guy.

Unique signatures are as much a part of show business (Michael Jackson's moonwalk) as they are a part of business. Experts, really, are just the show people of the business world. They see merit in the unique and the spectacular.

Unique signatures achieve a number of things. For starters, they are like the brand on the steer that identifies the owner. They are a signature; a means of pointing out that the work is yours. But they do more than just that.

They also show a distinct level of love and care for the work. Functionaries in a sweatshop generally don't care about their work. It's all about churning out volume quickly, and it is signed with a number, if that. But a unique signature shows the world that the worker is a craftsperson, an individual who takes pride in their work and cares profoundly about quality.

Because they understand this dynamic, top-level car manufacturers will sometimes have the name of a craftsperson signed on each engine of a limited sports car range. It adds exclusivity and hints at care.

So, how could you add a unique signature to your work? What are you known for, or what could you be known for? That distinction could help you to become, as Joe Calloway put it, a category of one. It could make your work stand out.

Often, a good starting point for discovering this one unique thing is to ask others who know and work with you to provide you with some thoughts and insights. They may be able to pinpoint your distinction better than you can.

If the answer is not readily apparent, don't worry too much. Just continue to pursue excellence. It will come with the passage of time. Your unique signature may also evolve as you develop and grow your own ideas about your work.

**Key question:**
What is your unique signature?

## 28. DEVELOP A UNIQUE FRAMEWORK PHILOSOPHY

This is one of the most important ideas that we will consider in expert positioning, and one which can be of great value to you.

If you take a look at the world's leading experts, you will often find they have a unique philosophy that they have turned into a framework. What is a framework? It is simply a way of organising and presenting your body of knowledge. It is, in other words, a novel and memorable *way of looking at things* – the packaging for your ideas.

The best frameworks can become sufficiently popular that people actually know you by your framework. *Rich Dad, Poor Dad*, for example, is a framework.

Leading experts have found a recognisable peg from which to hang their knowledge. Their framework may be the title of a book, but it also becomes a philosophy, a speech, a DVD, a TV show, seminar and more.

Think of these examples:

- Clem Sunter's series of Fox books, including *The Fox and the Hedgehog*, *The Mind of the Fox*, *Socrates and the Fox*, *Games Foxes Play*, and so on
- Stephen R. Covey's *The Seven Habits of Highly Effective People*
- *Blink* by Malcolm Gladwell
- The *Chicken Soup* series.

A different way of looking at the world (unique framework) makes you memorable, and makes it easier for others to identify and remember you.

Is your philosophy and message clearly stated and promoted through your website, marketing and so on? Is your distinction clear?

What makes you better or different? Frameworks are a big deal because the broad body of knowledge itself is available to everyone. But how you go about packaging that knowledge is what makes you unique.

It's particularly important when it comes to presenting your idea from a stage. Without an organising framework, the information in your presentation becomes just a series of loosely related platitudes. Have you ever experienced a motivational speech in which the speaker simply spouted a plethora of generic sayings, without any real cohesiveness or sense of direction? That's what happens when the framework is missing. There is no "glue", no "core". Without the framework, the speech descends into an unrelated set of random points. It lacks cohesion.

I have developed and used a number of frameworks over the years. One was called "hamster thinking". This is the intellectual space that I own and has become a part of my marketing and recognition factor. I have a number of motivational talks that address different issues using the hamster-thinking framework, such as: "Escape the Hamster Wheel" (a talk on personal initiative), "The Hamster in the Machine" (a look at hamster thinking in corporate companies), "Hamsters in your Funnel" (a sales talk) and "Beware of the Hamster" (focusing on customer service).

Each talk uses the model of hamster thinking as its basis, its skeleton, its essential *framework*, and then explores content from this framework outwards. It's a great organiser or anchor, and it's also nice in the sense that it is an easy visual to remember. "What does Douglas Kruger do?" "Oh, he talks about hamster thinking." That's my theme. That's my framework.

I recently watched a sales talk in which the presenter had no framework. He had simply cobbled together as much content as he could find, and loosely titled it a "sales seminar". It would have been easy to have given this mish-mash of ideas a more rigid framework. For instance, he might have called it "The 7 Mistakes Sales People Make". That's a framework. Or how about "6 Principles the World's Leading Sales Experts All Agree On"? That's a framework too.

We got to chatting about this after his talk, and I pointed out to him that he, as the presenter, gets to make an executive decision about how to organise his framework. That's because there are no rules here. You can make your own judgement call, and confidently declare that your talk features "The 9 Most Critical Lessons in Sales that You Have to Learn If You Ever Want to Drive that Mercedes".

That's a framework.

South African sales trainer Paul Naidoo labels his content "Sell Like an Indian"!

Conversely, I am continually impressed by how bodybuilding magazines manage to find frameworks, seemingly pulling them out of thin air, month after month. Let's be honest; how many times could you find different ways to frame and position basic information on workout routines?

Yet they somehow find new ones all the time. In one month's edition, they had a six-page feature on "The T-shirt Workout: How to Fill Out Your T's for Summer", right alongside a piece on "German Volume Training", and then a segment on "Exercises that Blast Body Fat". Another edition featured "The Ten Ton Workout" and "Book-end Training".

So, can you take your content, your knowledge and expertise, and organise it into a unique framework? Something that is exclusively yours? Something memorable, novel and easy to "get" quickly?

The key is that it should be very easy for prospective clients to understand. Nothing convoluted. Just a quick framework that says, "It's all about *this*". *Rich Dad, Poor Dad* certainly fits that bill: here is a series of lessons I learnt about wealth, from one man who was rich, and one man who was poor.

If you can organise it in such a way that their immediate response is, "I get it, and that's pretty cool!", then you know you are on the right track. If you can make it something visual, so much the better.

Remember, also, that the particular framework you use will determine the kind of visuals you *can* use. For instance, with my hamster speech, I can draw on the entire world of hamsters, with all its elements, such as cages, hamster-wheels and so on. I can show photos of hamsters with thought bubbles coming out of their heads. I can use hamster-wheels to make a point. It's all very quirky and memorable.

**Key question:**
When it comes to your unique framework philosophy, is there a way of organising your mountain of dots 'n dashes into something that people can instantly "get"?

## 29. MANAGE POPULARITY BY DESIGN

In PR terms, popularity means becoming the most viewed, the most sought after, the bestselling, the most prominent, best known and so on.

It is the career equivalent of being the popular kid. So let's ask some difficult but perfectly relevant questions: what exactly was it that made that annoyingly good-looking kid at school so popular? It's not all that hard to break the notion of popularity down into constituent parts. Let's start with that kid at school.

Chances are, they *were* good looking. After that, you will probably agree that they were highly visible. They had a lot to say about things. They were seen, regularly, with all the other cool kids, at all the important places. They seemed so self-assured, and everybody just *liked* them. Even the kids who didn't like them knew who they were. They were always getting up to things, getting involved in small dramas and scandals, being seen, heard, noticed. They were, in some way, *fabulous, larger-than-life* individuals.

Does any of that sound like it could be emulated? Of course it can. All of it!

Let's look at those qualities again, this time in the context of becoming an industry expert:

- *They are good looking:* Do you take care of your appearance and cultivate a look that makes a statement? Do you dress for strength and style, or do you look like somebody's nice auntie, or that friendly old uncle from the farm?
- *They are always highly visible:* Are you in the media, attending the events, socialising and being seen as you should?

- *They have a lot to say about things:* Come on, you're an industry expert, right? So how do you *feel* about the way things go? Do you see a case for change? Have you seen things that could be done differently? Better? Do you know what the regular problems are? Then you do have something to say.
- *They are seen with the right people at the right places:* We have discussed agents and editors, key players and high-ups. Meet them. Get to know them. Go to the events that they attend.
- *They are self-assured:* Do you speak confidently? How's your body language? Are you perceived as a confident go-getter?
- *People like them:* What active steps could you take to become liked in your industry? Are there underlings you could help? Overlords you could impress? Are you consistently courteous and warm? Do you have an aura and a vibe of energy and drive? Are you basically interesting?
- *They are always getting up to things:* In your world we call this thought leadership. Venture opinions. Get published. Speak in public. Create drives and initiatives. Interact with those who matter. Be a doer.
- *They create drama:* In your drives and initiatives, don't just do the dry, obvious thing. Factor in a little entertainment. Be a bit of a maverick. Add sizzle. Stand out on purpose.
- *They get seen, heard and noticed:* Insist on it. Because your reputation as an expert depends on it!
- *They are fabulous, larger-than-life individuals:* Get out there and glow!

## USE THE POWER OF VISUALS

You could say, "I'm a rock star". Or you could show a high-gloss, wide-angle poster of yourself on stage in front of thousands of screaming fans. Which do you think would be more effective?

As part of your expert positioning, be sure to get photographed, filmed, drawn and quartered ... or rather, *recorded*. Organise photos of yourself at high-level events, surrounded by lots of people.

Here is a simple trick that I learnt while speaking in Hong Kong. After my session, a cameraman directed me to go and stand in the middle aisle, surrounded by the audience on either side. He then asked the audience members to throw their hands in the air in a

Mexican wave. The resulting photo, of me standing upright, in the middle of 500 people seated and waving their hands, is spectacular to say the least. I use this photo as often as I can. I even added it to my email as a banner head. It says, "Here is a serious practitioner" more effectively than I ever could with words.

In addition to action shots like this, organise some high-quality static studio shots in various states of dress, from formal to casual, to use as biography photos and press release visuals.

Be aware that the variety of photos you have also adds credibility. For this reason, organise a quick photo shoot at every event that you do. The more photos you have of you plying your trade, the more serious a contender you appear.

If the nature of your work lends itself to doing so, photograph the work itself too. We often distinguish between an amateur and an expert on websites simply by the sheer volume of photographs of their work. It's a very basic psychology, but a very effective one: more photos equal greater credibility.

If the nature of your work does not lend itself to visuals, simply organise photos of yourself shaking hands with people in front of their buildings or company logos. But photos taken "in action" are always more effective. And you can find creative ways of going about it too. Mike Rowe, the presenter of *Dirty Jobs*, has various cleverly conceived publicity photos, which are easily found on a Google search, showing him wearing a suit, but carrying a spade over his shoulder, or covered in mulch and smiling sweetly.

The more visually iconic your photos are, and the more they tell an interesting story, the more iconic the perception of you will be. And you don't want to be a black-and-white corporate mug shot. You want to be a quirky visual icon. Make sure your photos have *splash*!

Also, make sure that you (or a service provider) can upload new photos on to your website on a regular basis, and add your new photos to your social media sites as often as you can. Strive to get to the point where an "Images" search for your name on Google will bring up page after page of your face.

I even like to go so far as to make little digital "posters" with my own pithy sayings or motivational quotes, which I can then circulate on Facebook and Twitter. I make them available as free downloads on my website, in order to promote myself visually through social media, and in order to achieve a greater visual presence when searched online.

**Key question:**
What visual or graphic opportunities could you exploit to create greater presence and visibility?

## 30. GAIN EXTRAORDINARY VISIBILITY

I've described the value of getting visibility in all the right places: regular columns in publications, interviews in the relevant industry media and so on.

However, from time to time, it is worth your while to do an extraordinary visibility stunt ... something that's more than just your regular article or your average interview ... something completely *out there*. Something spectacular. And what does spectacular mean? In the world of positioning, spectacular means: *newsworthy*.

You could, for example, attempt to set a new world record. A motivational speaker friend of mine who lived in Zimbabwe once set about breaking the world record for the longest motivational speech, which, if memory serves me, turned into an event lasting well over 24 hours. This was quite a clever move on his part, and he made sure that he organised all the appropriate media coverage. This earned him an "est" title.

You could even arrange sponsors for such an event, offering them publicity in return.

What can you do that is the "most" in your sphere? The biggest, the longest, the cleverest, the weirdest, the greatest, the shortest, fattest, highest, lowest, flattest or most incredible? What can you do that is visually appealing, or that has a certain storyline to it, or that touches people's heartstrings, or that just looks flat-out impressive? Even if your industry is fairly dry (check that, *especially* if it is), what would *just be too cool for words*? The sort of thing that leaves people saying, "Oh, wow! You're that guy who ..."

**BOOST YOUR SALES**

Visibility is a beginning and not an end in itself. It should always lead to more sales or business opportunities for you. Expos are always a good way to judge how proactive marketing people are about sales. Occasionally, they will have spectacular display stands, even including live entertainment, but there will be no visible example of the end product, and no direct way to purchase it. When you exhibit, display your end product clearly, and make it easy to purchase from you. Create a clear channel from interest to purchase.

**Key question:**
If you were a journalist, what sort of publicity event would hook your interest?

## 31. UNIFY THE TONE OF YOUR BRANDING AND COMMUNICATIONS

Large corporations are fastidious about their brands to the point where employees can't even design their own PowerPoint slides. Individuals operating on their own, and gradually emerging as industry experts, tend not to be as fussy. And it's to their detriment.

What tends to happen is that when you start your business, you get a friend to design a small but functional website. It looks decent. Your friend has decided on all the colours, the fonts and the total look and feel. Then you go and order business cards. And they have a different look and feel. You develop a little biographical document to give to clients. Different again. Eventually, you have an operational business that is utterly disparate in the branding tone of its own internal elements. In other words, you are advertising an amateur business.

I realised that this was the case with my own business about eight years into it! *Eight years*! My website didn't match my cards, my biography didn't match my email banner head – everything was running off on its own mission, singing its own little song.

Worse still, my website looked like a funky, friendly sort of place where this nice young kid advertised his home-based hobby. With that kind of branding, you can *never* command big money.

When I re-angled my branding so that all the elements matched, I decided to go for a very high-end feel. I do not want to look funky. When I described what I wanted to my web designer, I referred to the very clean, very expensive looks of some of the high-end fashion brands. Those who would typically make use of large white spaces, with a tiny dash of red somewhere on the page, or large black spaces with a simple element tastefully highlighted here and there. That looked exceptionally professional, and rather powerful, to me, and that was the image that I wanted to convey in turn.

A warm and fuzzy website may be nice if you are a home industry company – a *mom 'n pop* show – but portraying *mom 'n pop* to the world could relegate you to the lower rungs in your industry. So make the change away from it quickly. Position yourself as strongly and as professionally as possible. Your fees depend upon how you are perceived, and how you are perceived depends largely upon your branding. You do not want the people who pay you to think, "small fry".

Study how the top-end brands go about it. There is a very simple test. Low-end brands tend to shout. Top-end brands speak quietly and calmly, but with authority. This is true both of visual design, and of the degree of noise in television advertisements. The low-end brands have to scream at you for your attention. I fondly recall an advertisement for a BMW M3, in which there was no dialogue whatsoever. It simply ended with the slightest hint of a smile appearing on a man's face. Subtle. And powerful.

So, your website may say it in words, but does it say it in "feel"? Feel is more important. Strong look, strong visuals, decisive tone. Nothing scrappy or amateurish. Nothing that might be accused of being low-end.

If people have never heard of you before, but they stumble across your website while looking for the right person, their first impression, simply based on visual appeal, must be, "Wow! Impressive".

**Key question:**
How many of your marketing and communication elements currently have different branding tones?

## 32. CONTROL IMPORTANT POSITIONING SCENARIOS

I use the same Mediterranean barbershop every time I get a haircut. They do a good job and their fee is reasonable. I also like their confidence and professionalism, even if I can't understand half of what they say to me.

One day, however, I was subjected to the new trainee, freshly arrived from the mother country. Let me begin by saying that he actually did a really good job. The problem was, he didn't seem to think so.

He appeared tentative and unsure of himself, which made the experience tense and awkward. He also repeatedly apologised to me: for positioning my head at a convenient angle for him, for dropping a comb and for speaking to the other barbers in their native tongue.

Completely unnecessary. All he had to do was take charge – and I would have gone along with it. I *wanted* him to take charge. It was uncomfortable for me that he didn't do so.

Being an expert is like making love. If you are always uncertain, and always deferring to the other person, you actually become kind of boring. Take charge! Act with assured confidence. After all, you're good at this!

Are you under-confident in key scenarios? Or do you take charge and do what needs to be done? Decisively?

By now, you've noticed that there are a certain number of potential scenarios that are important for your positioning. They include meetings, interviews, speeches and public performances. These constitute your opportunities to be in the public eye, or to appear before your peers or clients, and to make an impression. *Impressions*, managed and accumulated over time, are the stuff experts are made of. Experts are nothing more or less than the sum total of public perceptions.

It stands to reason, then, that you should be completely in control of such scenarios.

This implies a few things. Let's start with the basics ...

Firstly, you have to recognise these scenarios. When meeting with a new client for the first time, for example, you need to recognise that this has the potential to be a career-defining moment. You need to prepare accordingly. Have you considered everything? Have you researched their background? Have you brought accompanying documentation? Are you properly dressed? Do you have sufficient handouts for more than the one person whom you assume you will be meeting? Do you have your diary on hand in case they ask about availability? Are you in every way prepared to do business?

Do you know a little about what is happening in their industry at the moment? Do you have tangible, physical examples of your product, or a way to demonstrate clearly your service so as to make it visual and real to them?

And these are just the questions you need to ask before a meeting. There are even more things to consider before a big speech or media appearance.

Your next consideration is psychological. You need to be emotionally in control and act decisively. You can't be a tentative Mediterranean barber and expect to be paid like an expert. You need the confidence to declare yourself the best choice for their needs.

In order to feel sure about yourself, always arrive well ahead of time. Scope out the meeting room, media studio or speech venue. Change anything that doesn't suit what you want to achieve. Settle in and get comfortable. Familiarise yourself with your surroundings.

Test the equipment. Ask any questions that you need to ask. Get what you need from this scenario. Take ownership of the event.

Next it's time to think politically: what is your agenda for this function? In addition to looking confident, have you decided the steps you will take, what content you will deliver and what messages you will put forward to further that objective? What's in it for your reputation? If you're there to sell, that's a surface-level agenda. Your deeper agenda may be to build a long-term relationship with a client. A good speech is just a surface-level agenda. The deeper agenda may be to position yourself as a future leader. Consider what you want to get out of important positioning scenarios, and boldly act accordingly.

When you are the one setting up and running any sort of positioning scenario, your control needs to be even greater. The ease, calm and authority with which you host these events will contribute to the overall slick impression you create.

When I host training for an organisation, I arrive a couple of hours ahead of schedule. This allows me to set up, deal with technical issues and generally get my act together. When my delegates arrive, I have name cards for each of them, I'm relaxed and personable and I can assume command in a friendly but confident way. It has become my space and I'm emotionally and psychologically in charge.

**Key question:**
What is your deeper agenda during important expert-positioning scenarios?

## 33. DO WHAT YOU SAY YOU WILL DO

One of the world's greatest credibility boosters is doing what you say you will do. In other words, be true to your word. Keep your promise.

This is inarguably the mark of a true professional. Not only that, but it is universally recognised as *the* sign of a quality human being. As one of the oldest and most revered values of the human race, this one is like a golden ticket to the esteem of others. Be true.

Of course, it's also hard work. And it implies a two-prong approach: on the one hand, once you have agreed to do something, you should do it; on the other hand, you shouldn't agree to do anything you don't believe you will do. It's a sign of immaturity to say yes to every request just because you hate to disappoint people. You will just disappoint by not holding true to your commitment. You have to be selective. Sometimes, saying no is a sign of maturity.

And it's often the simple things that really count here: returning a call, finding the contact details that someone requested, sending that email that you promised. The important thing is to be consistent. Don't become known as the person who doesn't respond ... the person who is a constant frustration to deal with.

Of course, it applies to the big deal stuff as well. I know of at least two speakers who have disappointed their agents – the same ones who I work with – and been taken off their books as a result. Imagine the consequence of not doing what you said you would *once*, and losing *all* your future business from one revenue stream as a result!

In my industry, that constitutes career suicide. These speakers should have done everything in their power to woo their agents back.

I can tell you that they didn't. And in this way, careers are made and broken. Professionals are born and abolished.

Be true to your word. The alternative is not worth it.

**Key question:**

If you're honest with yourself, when last were you *not* true to your word?

## 34. BE THE ONE WHO RESPONDS

Let's go one step beyond doing what you say you will. Let's look at the idea of turning "response" into a proactive technique that actually sets you apart.

Sounds simple, but it's a big deal. One of my agents once confided in me that she uses me on a regular basis, instead of other equally skilled speakers on her books, just because I respond more rapidly and more professionally. This means I'm making more sales, and earning more as a result of this concept, and this makes it an expert positioning technique.

A big part of the perception of professionalism is based on whether and how swiftly you turn around your communications. So always check and return emails and voicemail, even if you have to do it late in the evening. Of course, *immediately* is better than late in the evening. I can't count the number of times I have emailed multiple service providers asking for quotes, only to give the sale to the person who responded quickest. Equally, I can't count the number of times that two out of three service providers just didn't bother to respond at all. That's pathetic. And that puts you one business transaction down on your competitors and damages your brand.

Also, don't assume that you know what a person wants. Just because you see a missed call from "that guy", don't assume that you know what the message might be.

I made that mistake once (ironically, with the same agent who's usually impressed by my communication), when I believed she wanted to chat about a certain issue. At the time, we had a large corporate client who had been treating us in an unethical manner. I received my agent's text message asking me to give her a call. Instead of calling back, I wrote an email expressing my views on the matter and then carried on with my life. Three days later, she called me, pointing out that she had a completely different assignment that she'd been wanting to discuss with me. My hesitation in returning the initial communication meant I'd compromised my chances of landing the new assignment, and annoyed my agent. Bad move.

**Key question:**
Are you in the habit of returning all communications quickly?

## 35. MAKE THE OTHER LOOK GOOD

As an expert, it's very likely that you'll end up dealing with enablers. Enablers are people who help to grow your career and reputation, including agents, editors, speakers bureaus, legal representatives or high-level advocates in your industry, who may be called on to recommend the right name. Enablers can even be, and often are, the PA in the company to which you sell. You'd be amazed how many deals have been lost because the "expert" annoyed the PA!

Enablers are also the public and your family and friends. People who may freely choose whether or not to recommend you. After all, it is your job to earn your place at the end of the question, "You know who you should talk to about that?"

Each of these characters is a unique human being with wants and needs. They are equal-parts gatekeeper and springboard. They can help your career and, equally, they are capable of doing great damage to it.

Good relationships with these people are extremely important, and should be cultivated by design. Be good to them. Always do your best to make them look good. Often they are not your client per se, so your intention should be to make them look professional in the eyes of the end client. Empower and enable them. The more you are able to help them with their career goals, the more readily they will use you.

Once again, you are cultivating your name as the logical answer to the question, "You know who you should talk to?", and that cultivation should be taken seriously.

Similarly, if you deal with media, make their job easy by giving concise, useful information in a timely manner. If you deal with a bureau, give them all the materials and assistance they need to impress potential clients. Find ways to make your enablers' jobs easier, and to make them look good in the eyes of those with whom they deal.

Start by asking them what they need.

Create a situation where it simply makes sense to deal with you because you are clearly the best and you make them look good too. You make their job so easy!

I make it a habit to try to meet with a client whenever my agency asks about my availability for an event. On a few occasions, my willingness to meet and discuss their needs has been a deal-clincher for me. And it doesn't always require a meeting. Sometimes it's as simple as offering to call and let them hear your voice. This simple act changes you from a recommendation on a piece of paper to a personality they feel they know. It also shows that you are proactive, which in itself might be enough to tip the scales in your favour.

**Key question:**
What can you do to make your enablers look good in the eyes of their clients?

## 36. BE POLITICALLY ASTUTE

After a few years of interaction, you will find that your industry is surprisingly small. So don't slander anyone! Politics can make or break you.

Idle talk can come back to bite you in your dual cushions one day because agents talk among themselves, editors all know each other, and players in the industry meet and talk among themselves. Do anything to give yourself a bad name and you could actually ruin your entire business.

The converse is also true. Help others, offer your time, wisdom and advice, extend a helping hand and you will get a reputation for being quality. Reputation is everything for an industry expert.

In Toastmasters circles, there is a well-known story about a speaker who competed at the World Championships of Public Speaking, but showed a bad attitude when he didn't win the competition. He accepted his second-place trophy with a sour face and stormed off the stage. People still talk about the incident today! That speaker, realistically, has no hope of coming back and winning the contest. His reputation will forever cloud that possibility.

Bad political moves really do follow you. So be cautious, be sporting and be kind.

### RESPOND TO NEGATIVES QUICKLY AND MANAGE THE MESSAGE

There are whole books on how to handle negative media publicity. But if you are not going to read any of them, then at least take the time to watch a movie called *The Queen* starring Helen Mirren. This part-movie, part-biography shows what happens when you fail to answer the media. It uses as an example the British royal family's response, or lack thereof, to Princess Diana's death.

You and I will probably never deal with anything on that level. But it highlights how a complete communications lockdown during a disaster is never a good idea.

When anything happens to harm your reputation, seek a platform to address it quickly. But be smart about your response. Don't speak until you have really considered your response and, in particular, don't attack back. Your response should come across as concerned and professional, not adversarial. This applies even if you are under attack.

Let's take as an example a feud between two of the world's leading ... oh, I don't know ... ice sculptors! Harry the ice sculptor is interviewed on TV, and says nasty things about Joe the ice sculptor. He impugns his honour, his skill and the sharpness of his sculpting tools. If you're Joe, an equally nasty retaliation, tempting as it may be, will solve nothing. It will simply make you both look bad, and bring the ice sculpting industry into disrepute.

A better response would be something like this: "I am saddened by Harry the ice sculptor's words earlier today. I have always been a big fan of Harry and I highly respect his work. This is why it is surprising to me that a fellow ice sculptor would choose to speak as he did. Rest assured, I will not be impugning my fellow artist in any way whatsoever, and continue to be an ardent admirer of his work."

Full stop.

As a consequence, you, Joe the ice sculptor, now look like the bigger man! You have retained your professional credentials. Harry looks like a bit of a twit.

That's how it's done.

**Key question:**
Does negative media put you into a state of emotional lockdown, or do you seek out the opportunity in the storm?

## 37. PRICE YOURSELF AT THE RIGHT LEVEL

A great many entrepreneurs actually undercharge, and it hurts them badly.

Position yourself as the cheap alternative and, ironically, you may find yourself doing less business. This is because people largely judge value and quality based on price, which, in turn, is why Mercedes hasn't gone broke in spite of its galactic pricing.

Don't do miniscule profit margins. You are only hurting yourself. Practise healthy profit margins that recognise and reflect your input and expertise, and which create the right market perception.

The concept of *value* is everything for the industry expert. Increase your value, or increase the value of what you offer, and you can earn more money over less working hours.

Offer low-value labour, and you will earn less money over more working hours. This single epiphany is *the* difference between the labouring classes, who never break even, and the professional and entrepreneurial classes, who ultimately outstrip their debt and become wealthy. It is one of the great markers separating worker from expert.

**MISIDENTIFYING A PROBLEM**

In 2011, I started bumping my head against a new problem. I was becoming busier than one person can handle. The nature of my work is such, though, that it is difficult to outsource. When you run a burgeoning beauty salon, you can hire more beauticians. When you deliver keynote speeches on your own specific skill set, telling your own specific stories, the load becomes more difficult to spread.

For a long while I agonised over possible solutions (virtual PAs, small support teams and time-management courses). But when I read Alan Weiss's book, *Million Dollar Speaking*, and learnt that this incredibly prosperous man gets by without any support staff, it occurred to me that my thinking was entirely wrong. I was in need of a Copernican Revolution.

My problem was that I was trying to apply the labourer's concept of how to get richer, which is: push your wheelbarrow for more hours.

## EXPANDING YOUR SCOPE IS NOT NECESSARILY THE ROAD TO WEALTH

"Carry more bricks to earn more coins." This is classic working-class thinking. I don't mean this in any elitist sort of way; it is simply a fact. Day labourers, when not coping with workload or prospering to the degree they feel they should, will strive to work longer hours, handle more and expand the scope of their labour. The thinking is oriented around "getting an extra coin". To achieve this, they might get a second job.

In simple terms, their philosophical approach is: more hours = more coins.

This thinking will keep you poor. It will also ensure that you burn yourself out. And it's completely wrong for the industry expert.

## THE COPERNICAN REVOLUTION

The solution is not to carry more bricks. The solution is to think completely differently. The solution, in fact, is to carry something that is *worth more* than bricks. In this way, your equation becomes: carry something more valuable over the same time period = receive more coins.

In my case, this meant a decision to position myself actively on a higher level as a speaker. It meant raising my fees and jettisoning my lower-paying, high-input clients.

Think of how elegantly such an approach solves the problem of capacity: do less work for more money. Instead of constantly scrambling for lots of low-end work, you are, at your leisure, taking on fewer, higher-paid assignments.

This approach in no way advocates laziness. It takes a great deal of work to hold your position at the top end of the market. But it will mean less consumption of time for higher reward, and that is a meaningful goal.

People often respond to this line of thinking with the question: "What if they can't afford me?" The answer is painfully simple: then they are not your customer. If you are constantly talking to people who can't afford the premium offer, then you are marketing yourself to the wrong customer base. Aim for the high end. Let the entry-level practitioners have the low end. You own the premium space, and charge accordingly.

Of course, you have to be worth it.

Positioning is an art. It is the art upon which this entire book focuses. And the danger is that you are simply seen to be overcharging for an inferior product. That's a bad idea. Not only is it unethical, but it only takes two or three clients getting burnt before the word gets out and your business falters.

No, you have to actually *be* the quality for which you charge. But if you *are* the Mercedes Benz of your industry, you *are entitled to charge a premium*. And your market will expect it and pay it.

It's an interesting build-on-build dynamic: the more you put your price up, the more you will be seen as a quality offering. The higher the quality of your offering is, the more you can put your price up.

So if you have hit a ceiling of income-to-capacity, and want to earn more, consider whether you are simply trying to carry more bricks. There are smarter approaches.

Here are three suggestions for how to choose better positioning over more hours carrying bricks:

## 1. Fire your low-paying, high-input clients

They are a drain on your time, they are not worth the financial reward, and perhaps most importantly, their high visibility in your own consciousness will keep you believing that you operate at that level. After all, if you see them often, they are your norm. Give them up to the entry-level operators. Own the top end of the market.

If you are having difficulty with this idea, think about it this way: doing one job for 30 coins is worth more than doing three jobs for 10 coins each. How do I reach this seeming mathematical impossibility? Well, each job implies a certain amount of cost. If you do one job for 30 coins, you will incur one cost. If you do three jobs for the same amount of money, you will be down by three instances of cost. Doing less work for more money is exponentially more lucrative.

## 2. Dump the bricks and carry gold

What do you offer that is high input and low-yield? Are you scrambling to sustain the small profit margin part of your business? It's time to dump it and focus on the high-yield stuff. You don't have to be all things to all people. I repeat: you don't have to be all things to all people. You may focus on the high-margin stuff. It's your career. It's your life. Rather be the thing that generates high income.

## 3. Increase your fees

Raise your fees. Raise your quality concurrently. Try to position your fees in the mid-to-upper cost range of your industry. Never position yourself in the lower cost range. If you do, you become a commodity, which means that you are interchangeable. This is not clever positioning.

Ultimately, your goal is to be shopped on quality, not on price. If you are shopped merely on price, you are a commodity, and you are interchangeable. But if you are perceived as the expert in your industry, your cost is secondary. They have to have *you*.

**Key question:**
Are you charging at the mid-to-upper levels of your industry?

## 38. HAVE YOUR CUSTOMERS SELL TO YOU

Desperation. It is the hallmark of an amateur. And nowhere does it show its ugly, career-and-income limiting face more clearly than in the selling scenario.

An unconfident amateur will generally take any workload and make any promise for any fee. The workloads are usually very high and the fees very low. In this way, entrepreneurs tend to bankrupt themselves. They also lower the value of their brands.

As an expert, I would like you to approach the buying scenario differently. I want you to go into these situations with the attitude that your customers should prove to you that they have a sufficient problem to warrant your expertise. In other words, they should sell to you.

If their problem is sufficient, your response might be, "Yes, I believe I can help you."

This shift in mindset achieves a number of things:

1. It removes your desperation. You go into a meeting feeling that you have a valuable solution, which they need to recognise. They are buying a leading expert.
2. It prevents you from accepting damaging business, which is either outside your scope – and thus likely to go wrong and harm your reputation – or too cheap to be worth your while. Without desperation, you are able to walk away when necessary, with a courteous smile and a "thanks for your time".
3. It actually benefits the client because it means that the emphasis during the discussion is not on how great you are, but on the severity and intricacies of their problem. The better you understand their

problem, the more ably and specifically you can solve it and delight your customer. Also, the more time you spend focusing on their problem, the more professional (and the less desperate) you appear.

Getting your potential clients to focus on and explain the severity of the problem that led to their contacting you in the first place is also an excellent selling technique. It reignites the buyer's pain and gets them emotionally involved in the solution. It also allows you to evaluate the worthiness of the assignment as they speak.

It is a good basic sales technique to start with their pain, rather than starting with your accomplishments. Go into the meeting with the confident (but never smug) idea that they need to sell their problem to you. They need to convince you that they warrant your services. If you feel they qualify, you can then make yourself available. If they don't, you won't.

What a sense of power over your own destiny!

**Key question:**
Do you sell from a place of desperation?

## 39. GIVE GUARANTEES

Whenever I quote for a training session in presentation skills, I give a simple guarantee that adds value to the total price. I guarantee that anyone who has been on my course can always ask me any questions they may have about presenting via telephone or email. I offer this as a lifetime guarantee to each delegate, even if they should leave the organisation.

Companies are impressed by these guarantees, and I repeat them verbally to my delegates at the end of a day's training. They are a spectacular show of faith in what I offer, and a way of easing the client's nerves about spending large amounts with me.

Interestingly, I have yet to have anyone – even one single individual – take me up on my guarantee. So setting it up has not resulted in floods of additional work. But it's there. And it's a part of my positioning.

Clients are reassured by guarantees. They convey a subliminal message that the seller, or expert, has absolute confidence in the quality of his or her product, or his or her capacity to perform. And this removes a barrier to purchase.

What guarantees could you give for what you do professionally? Guarantees are comforting for those who must spend money to use your skills. They create trust, they show your confidence in your own work, and they reduce your clients' perception of risk in the transaction. They allow you to charge more because you clearly stand by your work and guarantee their satisfaction.

Be careful, however, about providing full money-back guarantees on completely subjective grounds ("if you're not happy") as you may have to live up to them to your own detriment.

**Key question:**
Could your guarantee be in some way more impressive than your competitors'?

## DESIGNING YOUR MESSAGE

So far we've looked at an array of things you can do to position yourself as an expert. Implied in a great many of them was the idea of using events, meetings, media and other opportunities to communicate the right messages and perception. In the remaining ten ways to position yourself as an expert, I will explore the idea of the message itself, and show you some structuring skills that will set you apart and make your messages memorable.

You may need to design your message for many reasons: speeches, interviews, articles or copywriting for your own marketing materials. In each case, you want to be a high-impact communicator in this career-enabling scenario.

Most speeches are low impact. They are drenched in mind-numbing bullet points, and focus on facts, rather than messages. As an expert, I would like you to reverse that concept. You should be high impact. You should do messages, not data dumps. You can add a smattering of facts to support your messages, but strong messages are the key. You are telling them what to think. And you are simply supporting your ideas with a fact or two.

You should also "speak strong", a phrase used by international speaker and author, Randy Gage. Randy, who is very highly paid and a frequently booked speaker, asserts that "safe speak" will only get you so far. Beyond a certain point, he contends, you have to stop craving the need for everyone's approval and become a leader. You have to have a strong point of view and speak with authority.

Of course, this implies a balancing act ...

## START BY UNDERSTANDING THE DIFFERENCE BETWEEN CONFIDENT AND SMUG

A big part of expert positioning is confidence. It takes confidence to write an article, deliver a speech, or grant an interview in which you tell people what to do and think, using a strong point of view. But it is important. Remember that Personality is one part of the big three that make up an expert (along with Knowledge and Sustained Publicity). But personality needn't be brash or crass. There are many gentle personalities making a huge impact in their respective industries.

So let's take a moment to look at the difference between confidence and smugness.

There's nothing worse than that smug adolescent who practises one-upmanship ...

"You've been overseas? Well, *I've* been to every country on the planet! You drive a Porsche? Well, *I* taught Michael Schumacher everything he knows! You're the chairperson of the European Union? *I'm* the head of an intergalactic empire poised to take over the universe!"

... So there!

We all know someone who does it.

And curiously, despite their desperation to look like the big cheese, they just wind up looking silly and juvenile. Experts are more mature than that.

Smug is not a winning attitude. Interestingly, most top performers are generally quite humble, personable human beings, who don't need to brag about their accomplishments. This is because they understand the difference between genuinely being the best and the counterfeit nature of bragging.

Yes, I did state earlier that you should be declarative about your position as an expert. But it's not the same thing as being a bragging teenager. You do it as a calm, controlled and experienced veteran, and you are simply stating a fact. There should be no desperation in your statement: "I r*eally* am the best! *Really, really! If you don't believe me, I'll hold my breath!*"

Experts are humble, but they can state their good qualities calmly and honestly.

With this in mind, let's look at some specific ways to make your messages stronger.

**QUICK TIP**

The next time you have an opportunity to design a message, be it writing an article or facing an interview, why not reread these chapters before getting started?

## 40. START WITH A TOOLBOX

When you consider your own brand and the way in which you represent yourself to the world, what are the associations that spring to mind?

Let's look at this idea in terms of car brands.

Would you peg yourself as a Mercedes Benz? ... or a Ferrari? ... a Smart Car or a Subaru?

Manufacturers don't use anything even close to the same terminology when advertising their brands. Terms like "premium", "luxury" and "sophistication" will appear, consistently and intentionally, in Mercedes Benz adverts, on its websites and in its outgoing communications. Subaru rhetoric will lean toward phraseology like "sporty", "rally heritage" and "outstanding performance". These are values that accentuate sportiness rather than refined luxury.

Even when Mercedes *does* talk about power and performance, for instance, in the rhetoric around its AMG models, it aims for a different feel, using phrases like "masterful performance" and "a perfect blend of power and design".

Same essential ideas. Completely different positioning.

Yet the subtle distinction is achieved through the selection of words. These brands put a lot of work into distinguishing themselves, and they have a verbal toolkit as part of their arsenal for doing it.

So, what phrases describe you? What words should appear regularly in your branding and communication? Write them down in the form of a list. They are your toolkit, and you can draw upon them whenever you need to.

Here are a few suggestions for the type of thing you might include on your list:

- Premium
- Pre-eminent
- The leading authority in ...
- Widely published
- Well established
- Longest running
- Most energetic voice to appear on the scene in decades
- Class-leading.

Of course, if your brand is creative, and your company is, for example, an X-games eventing group, you might use terms like:

- The wildest force in the nation
- Always pushing the boundaries of physical possibility
- No holds barred
- Biggest
- Baddest
- Bangin'est and so on.

Design your terminology toolbox to fit your brand feel, and carry on adding to it as you gain a greater understanding of who and what you are. Once you have your list, how should you go about using it?

Let's stick with our example and assume that you were representing a luxury car dealer in a media interview. You might answer a question by beginning with the phrase "As the leading authority in automotive excellence, our organisation believes that ..."

Let's say you're heading up a feisty, start-up computer company. If you were writing an article, you might write, "As the most energetic new voice in this industry, our view is that ..."

The terminology toolbox provides you with a list of go-to phrases that capture your precise marketing message quickly and succinctly. Under pressure, you can fall back upon them and be sure that you will get your message through. You can be talking about something else entirely, but drop these little phrases in from time to time. Like verbal soldiers, they will go to battle and do your marketing for you.

**Key question:**
Are the key marketing phrases in your terminology toolbox catchy and memorable?

## 41. DETERMINE SOME PASSION POINTS

Want to be noticed? Want to be seen as a passionate practitioner in your industry? Then how about championing a cause? Want to *lose* customers? Fail to identify the cause that is already built into your business.

BBC television once featured a show called *Mary, Queen of Shops*. The premise was simple: Mary, a business consultant, would go into failing stores and turn them around, using business acumen and common sense to return them to profitability.

In one episode, Mary went into the store of a lady who sold clothes to full-figured women. The store was failing dismally, despite a sizeable (ha-ha) market. Mary spent a little time observing her and made two discoveries:

1. The owner of the store had a second job as a fitness instructor at a gym.
2. She disdained what she called "fat" people.

Consequently, two things happened. The first is that she spoke to her client base in condescending terms, saying things such as, "This will help you to hide the rolls of fat sticking out here," and worse.

But secondly, and perhaps more importantly, she failed to exploit the PR value of the cause that was built into her store.

Consider: making full-figured women elegant and beautiful is not just an industry. It is a cause. It comes with attendant emotions and a requirement for loads of input and information. And if you are a thought leader in this sphere, who also owns a shop catering to full-figured women, they *will* come to you. They will do so because you are "for" them; you are for their cause. What a great excuse for a platform, and what a perfect win-win situation.

Your communications can benefit immensely from the use of a cause, which is a powerful rallying point.

Few things define a brand more distinctly than their causes and campaigns.

For me, as a presentation skills trainer, I am militantly anti-PowerPoint. I can (and do) speak passionately about how reliance on PowerPoint leads to lazy presenters, creates staccato deliveries, and is counterproductive to most presentation goals.

As a five-times national public speaking champion, I can do this. I get to make authoritative pronouncements on what is, and what is not, preferable because of my perceived expertise.

Audi punts the merits of four-wheel drive, while BMW, equally passionately, punts the values of rear-wheel drive. These days, both brands speak about being leaders in fuel-efficiency.

Passion for a cause changes you from a vague practitioner to someone who takes a specific stance. Built into the notion of taking a stance is the implied idea that you're *qualified* to take this view, which positions you as an expert. Hence, a stance is a powerful thing.

Companies that might otherwise appear to their public as mere grey buildings, doing vague business things beyond the reach of mere mortals, become more *specific*, more d*efined*, when they are militantly anti-global warming (a boringly obvious but apparently popular cause), or passionately pro-sports development. You might be the animal expert, who campaigns against the docking of dog's tails. This makes you a specific entity, a passionate practitioner with beliefs, rather than just an animal expert. It also changes the perception of you from *someone who works in the industry* to *someone who is passionate about the industry.* Those two designations are worlds apart, and you should go for the latter.

So what cause should you choose?

Politicians know that such hot topics can determine the rise and fall of leaders. Fortunately, as you grow your own expert status, you don't have to negotiate the minefields of abortion, gay marriage and so on. But the very idea of standing for a cause, any cause, is a useful communications tool, and such passion points make you media-worthy.

Beware, though, not to take a stance that can isolate you from your market. For instance, don't be the expert on cellphone technology and then speak about the dangers of using cellphones. That's just not smart.

**PRACTICAL IDEA**

Causes create content. Are you keen on developing your media presence? How about having a show, column or regular magazine feature relating to your cause?

TV channels like BBC Learning and The Style Network are largely based on "cause" content. With shows like *How to Look Good Naked*, *The Timid Girl's Guide [to Dating]* and *Peter Perfect*, presenters, who are considered experts in their fields, teach individuals how to "look good naked", "flirt effectively" and "properly market and position their businesses respectively".

**Key question:**
What issues are you strongly opposed to in your industry and how can they be turned into a rallying cry?

## 42. FIND AN OPPORTUNITY TO GIVE VALUE

When we hear terms like "value", we intrinsically feel we should agree with their ethos. They just *seem* right. But then comes the tricky part. How do you actually *create* value? How do you go about providing it, practically speaking? How do you use it in the media, and how can you apply it to sell more effectively than your competitors?

The simplest answer is: by providing useful education. Don't just preach, *teach*. And teach what? Teach them how to use you, and your organisation, to their benefit.

Let's start with media interviews.

Whether you are making yourself available to the media in a proactive way, or they have contacted you to ask for your input on an issue, find a way not only to give your comment, but also to maximise the opportunity by making it educational.

For example, let's imagine I'm the nation's best-known private detective. I make a killing out of snooping around in other people's business and a radio station has requested an interview with me. Their agenda is to ask me some questions about a recent celebrity scandal, and the role private investigators played in uncovering it. But *my* agenda is to position myself as the foremost private detective in South Africa. I want publicity and I want business. I want to expand my perceived stature.

So, here's how I'd do it ...

*Producer:* So, we'd really appreciate your insight on this topic. Could you come into the studio tomorrow and do the interview with our talk-show host?

*Me:* Sure, I'd be more than happy to. Tell you what, though, I believe I can offer you even more than that. How about if I also give you a small educational piece, just two minutes, on the most effective ways for individuals to go about using the services of private investigators? I'll cover the top five misunderstandings commonly held by the public.

*Producer:* Wow, sounds good. Thanks for that.

*Me:* (internal monologue): Teehee! I just offered him the opportunity to teach my customers how to use my services! Suh-weeet!

Don't just provide opinion. Provide useful knowledge. And make sure that the useful knowledge guides potential clients to you. Implied in the information should be the underlying message: *Real professionals* (like me) *do it this way,* or *the correct way to go about it* (in addition to getting coaching from a professional like me) *is this* ...

Now let's take a look at "value" in a sales scenario. Here's a quick snapshot of the evolution of sales from the dawn of time until now ...

Floating amoebas – prostitution – goods and services – selling the *benefits* of goods and services – selling *solution* – and finally selling *value.*

Congratulations. You are now qualified to talk knowledgeably about the complete history of sales. You slugger, you!

Let's discuss the latest one. Say you're marketing an events company. You can stand out from your competitors by teaching your customers how to host a successful event, including all the ins and outs. After all, you know much more about events than they do. You're the expert. You know what can go wrong, what they need to consider as they plan, what opportunities are available to them for additional marketing, the little tips 'n tricks that can help to set their event apart.

The simple act of pointing these things out – of *educating* them – is the true essence of value.

The best opportunity for distinction lies in how useful *you* are at guiding them toward their goals. That value is worth more to your clients than your actual product or service.

With this in mind, are you using value as part of your unique selling proposition? Is it built into your pitches? Do you have leave-behind materials with insightful tips for your customers on how to go about what they are trying to achieve (with the underlying message that you can help to get them there)?

PR practitioners do this all the time and it works. Dispense knowledge for free. Teach your customers how to achieve their goals. Show them how best to use you. Be proactive and guide them through the whole process like a caring host. *That* is value.

## EXCAVATE MEANING AND PROVIDE INSTRUCTION

The difference between a newspaper journalist and a newspaper columnist is this: the journalist reports facts, the columnist interprets facts. You need to think like a columnist.

This distinction can set you apart as a thought leader. Mere practitioners would only give facts about their industry. Thought leaders consider these facts, and then give meaningful interpretations of them. For example, they might take the facts at hand, and then suggest possible future outcomes.

Experts actually go one step further still. Rather than just give meaningful interpretations, they will suggest "what to do about it".

Let's say that you're a political analyst. A fairly mediocre analyst would take a look at the world scenario and then design a presentation in which they prove the idea: "China is expanding into Africa." Like a newspaper reporter.

A more advanced and expert analyst would use the approach: "What does China's expanse into Africa *mean* for local business?" In such a talk, they'd give well-considered and in-depth explorations of the meaning and results of the event. Like a columnist.

A top analyst would even go one step further, and tell the audience what to do about it.

This distinction is important for you as you position yourself not merely as a source of facts, but as a genuine thought leader. So are you presenting just the facts, or have you learnt to interpret and instruct?

**Key question:**
What free education can you give away with the underlying message that you're the best in the business?

# 43. USE THE THOUGHT-LEADERSHIP FORMULA

Let's say that you have secured that half-hour speaking slot that could enable you to remain in the industry consciousness for years. You know that your goal is to be the thought leader. You need to know how to handle it.

Let's begin with a few "thou shalt not's":

1. Thou shalt not speak to slides. That's for junior members of the sales team, who can't remember the company's name. Make a strong impression by knowing your content, connecting with the audience and delivering your speech without visible notes.
2. Thou shalt not do data dumps. This is all about creating impressions of strength and leadership, not about reciting every possible dot and dash in your litany of facts. Your message matters more than the facts that support it.
3. Thou shalt not indulge in long waffling "thank you's". Lists and formalities dilute your impact. Leave them for the MC. Speak strong.

## A DIFFERENT APPROACH

The nature of thought leadership presentations differs from speeches you've done in the past.

For starters, this is a presentation with a strong point of view. Don't try to be gentle, euphemistic or neutral. This is the forum for bold ideas, strong suggestions and a powerful sense of voice. Your brand will not benefit from an overly cautious presentation. I'm not suggesting you champion the death penalty or dance through the abortion minefield, but you should pioneer passionate views about your industry.

You should also bring a dash of something personal to the mix. If your goal is to stand out, there is nothing quite as unique as you.

**THE STRUCTURE**

Now let's get practical. Here is your basic structure for a thought-leadership presentation:

- Tell them how things used to be.
- Tell them what things they should be paying attention to now and why.
- Tell them what it means to them, including the pitfalls and opportunities.
- Tell them what things will work going forward.
- Tell them how things will turn out.
- Leave them with the implied message: "Follow me".

Follow this structure and you will create a strong impression. It contains all the nuts and bolts of a solid thought-leadership presentation, and plenty of room for your own personal interpretations.

Bear in mind, though, that this is merely an outline. Your task is to make it come alive, with humour, stories, word-pictures, metaphors and memorable phrases.

Thought-leadership presentations are immensely self-actualising. You get to use creative techniques to express your strongest opinions to an audience that will thank you for not playing it safe. You get to benefit their lives by telling them what you think they should do. Few things make you feel as alive.

Ultimately, they are about impressions. Speak with conviction. Speak strong. Own the stage and they will feel your energy.

**Key Question:**
Beyond simply having the facts, have you considered what your insights and information mean in the lives of your target audience?

## 44. SPEAK WITH STRENGTH

Brand confidence is reflected in your use of language. An important part of your language style should be to use the active rather than the passive voice. Learn how to strongly say rather than vaguely discuss.

What is the difference between active and passive voice? Here's a practical example:

- *Active voice:* James Brown wrote this book.
- *Passive voice:* This book was written by James Brown.

Here is another type of passive sentence: "The appropriate amount must be paid by the person buying the item." Written in the active voice, this sentence would read, "*You* must pay the appropriate amount when buying the item."

You can instantly see that writing in the passive tense is much more formal. It is also more academic and more difficult to understand. Its purpose is essentially to be euphemistic, to "soften" and avoid offending anyone. In other words, it is a way of speaking as though you are apologising for it. Experts don't work that way. Experts are sources of strength and guidance.

Passive tense and euphemisms are an all too common addition to modern political discourse, where the notion of addressing anybody directly is considered rude. The news on TV is awash with soggy phrases like "it was alleged", "whereas it was believed" and "measures are to be expected". The passive voice is an ineffective way of speaking, and often an avoidance tactic.

Look out for lines in your speeches like "it is believed", "an analysis is to be done" and "it shall not be the case that anyone will". Rewrite them so that responsibility is assigned to someone. For example, "I believe", "You must do an analysis" and "Please don't".

If you do not write your communications out word for word, you will need to apply this technique on the fly. It's not as hard as you might think. Keep these simple guidelines in mind:

- Speak as if you are instructing a single person.
- Avoid formal phrases or euphemistic language, such as "it should be noted that". Instead, say, "You should note". Talk *to* people, rather than softly tiptoeing around them.
- Ditch soggy, lifeless "political speak". Avoid phrases you hear on the news like "in terms of" or "it has come to light that", or "whereas it was previously the case that" and other such brain-numbers.

If you're going to say something, say it boldly and directly. Don't cloak it in verbiage. Authority comes from delivering language boldly, simply and with conviction – not from hiding your meaning like a slithering politician with a sinister agenda.

**SOUND BITES**

Another way to speak with strength is to use power phrases or sound bites. Sound bites are short, punchy phrases that are easily remembered and repeated. They are generally the small portion of a statement or speech that is played or quoted by the media as representative of what you were saying. When you see an ad for a popular documentary-style show, such as Nigella Lawson's cooking show, you will generally be shown a sound bite.

Your goal in using sound bites is to achieve what US speaker Brian Walter describes as "going verbally viral". You want your phrases quoted, used as tweets, inscribed upon memories, and in a best-case scenario, emblazoned as article headlines.

When George Bush, Sr said, "Read my lips: no new taxes," he created a memorable sound bite. So did Franklin D. Roosevelt when he declared, "The only thing we have to fear – is fear itself." Some are created quite by accident, as in Bill Clinton's "I did not have sexual relations with that woman". They survive (for better or worse) because they are powerful.

Sound bites are, in fact, so powerful that they may enter into the public consciousness and become part of our everyday speech. Hollywood tries to capitalise on the self-perpetuating power of sound bites by creating them for their characters. Phrases like "I'll be back" and "Show me the money!" spring to mind.

For your presentations, the repeated theme from your metaphor will work as a sound bite. But you're by no means limited to just that. You can have any number of sound bites in your speech; a clever turn of phrase here, a memorable line there.

You can create sound bites by:

- *Being dramatic:* "I have nothing to offer but blood, sweat, toil and tears."
- *Twisting a common phrase:* The cooking show that said, "This is a country with no time to stop and stir."
- *Making up a unique word:* "Is presenteeism hurting your business?"
- *Using alliteration:* As in the phrase "verbally viral" or "the wheelbarrow way".
- *Being novel:* "Now go crush the Cinderella in your financial thinking!"
- *Using musical phraseology:* "Never and never and never again … !"
- *Using interesting visuals:* "I hope to stir the custard in your cranium."

I have always loved the catchphrase "Stories are the medium of human communication". I use it often in my speaking and training.

I've also developed phrases like "hamster thinking" and "exorcising your inner hamster" appear in a lot of my articles, speeches and marketing materials.

Use a catchphrase or an interesting line repeatedly, and soon it will become your "thing".

Catchphrases can just be a cute and memorable thing you say, or, more desirably, they can be small key learnings. Point-makers.

Take my anti-PowerPoint campaign, for instance. The widely used phrase is "death by PowerPoint". This isn't just a memorable catchphrase, it is also educational. It makes a point.

If you were a financial expert and you wanted to use the idea of people dropping out of investments too early as your passion platform, you might want to call these people something derisive and memorable, such as "penny-scared early-dropouts". Perhaps you can think of something more memorable. Something that rhymes or uses alliteration. Something that sticks in the mind because of its interesting imagery ...

Perhaps you could even play with innuendo: "Why no one appreciates early withdrawal" ...

The concept of using interesting language to stand out is also not limited to sound bites. You can use it on product descriptions as well. An example that springs to mind is the "java jackets" on a Starbucks paper cup. Such clever and memorable wording. It makes use of alliteration, it makes the product human, it is visual and it is quirky.

**Key question:**

Based on issues in your industry, what catchphrases could you develop that sum up a concept quickly?

## 45. USE THE INCREDIBLE POWER OF METAPHORS

I'm an enormous and utterly devoted fan of metaphors and stories. I honestly believe that there are few tools in the entire sphere of communications more powerful or effective than those two. They are closely related, but I'll deal with them separately.

Let's start with metaphors. Metaphors are often described by communication specialists as "the highest form of communication". They cut through clutter and make a point quickly and vividly. Metaphors are a weapon and you would do well to add them to all your outgoing communication.

Using a metaphor, of course, is simply comparing one thing to another. It is certainly not a new idea, but it is an effective way of taking a complex, abstract notion and turning it into something that people can "see".

It's the difference between: "We're a small company competing against big-brand names" and "We're that four-foot nothing martial artist that takes on the six-foot boxers ... and flattens them all!"

You can use metaphors in your speeches, sales pitches, articles and interviews. You can use them in casual conversation whenever you tell people what you do. You can use them in arguments as you vie for your point to be heard and accepted. Use them whenever you need to *persuade*.

Metaphors get the job done quickly in addition to being novel and memorable. Here are some examples:

An American professional speaker describing what it's like to speak for the youth market: "You have to smuggle your messages in-between stories. You have to be like a motivational ninja!"

Chief Financial Officer of Barnard Jacobs Melllet, Mark Appleton: "This time last year, you were lost in the forest and you were afraid, and you turned to me for guidance. What you didn't know was that I was equally scared. But that wasn't good enough. So we dug deep, and pulled on a hundred years of experience, and sought real answers. We found a glimmer of light in one direction and led you that way. We're proud to say that we are now emerging from the forest, and the choice we made for you was the right one."

And a few gems from Jeremy Clarkson, the über-master of the modern metaphor, presenting on the motoring show "Top Gear":

"It was a bit like putting a sticking plaster on a leaking nuclear missile!"

"Look at the way it's shaped. It looks like a dog hunkering down to do its business."

"Most supercars make you feel like you're wrestling an elephant up the back stairs of an apartment building. But this one is like rubbing honey into Kiera Knightley!"

"This thing has so much torque, it could tear a hole in time!"

"It's about as feminine as a burst sausage!"

**Key question:**
Are you like the empty husk that never developed a metaphor?

## 46. STORIES ARE YOUR VERY BEST FRIENDS

Nothing appeals to the human mind like a well-told story. In the sphere of communication, it beats the spittle out of facts and data any time.

Think about this: the world's most enduring expert dispensaries, the great religious texts such as the Bible, make extensive use of stories, and Jesus's lessons were all delivered as parables (illustrative stories). Two thousand years later, their messages live on.

An instance of communication, be it a speech, an interview or an article, that makes no use of the most basic example or illustration lacks an anchor for its message. It becomes pure philosophy with no substance. If your audience is going to listen to you for any length of time, you need to give them *meat*. Stories are meat.

Another advantage of storytelling is that it can be very economical. Stories (just like metaphors) summarise complex points easily. Professional speakers often meet past members of an audience, who will say something like "I still remember that story you told about dropping yoghurt on your wife's new carpet and her *reaction*!"

They never say, "I remember the point you made about owning up to mistakes at home." No, they remember the *story*. And if they remember the story, they got the point.

Finding stories is not as difficult as it may seem. You can draw on small, amusing incidents from home or work ... just the ordinary stuff of life.

In order to make a point about the importance of work-life balance, one of my favourite US speakers, Jim Key, told a simple little story about arriving home to his young daughter after a hard day's work.

His daughter, tucked up in bed, asked him to sing the *Barney the Dinosaur* song. In his exhaustion, he lashed out at her and said, "I don't want to sing that silly song! You sing it if you want."

And she did. Through quivering lips and the beginning of tears, she sang, "I looove youuu, youuuuu loooove meeee ..."

This brought Jim to tears of his own and a swift apology to his little girl.

It's such a simple little story. But it tugged at the audience's heartstrings. And for that reason, they'll remember it, and they'll remember him.

And you can use a story like that to make all sorts of points. Let's say you're talking to a corporate group about a mistake your organisation has made. You could tell that story. And you could use it as an introduction to the idea that even the most caring guardians make mistakes from time to time. But all that matters is they learn from their mistakes, and your organisation plans to do just that.

See how it works? Simple stories that illustrate principles.

Start to collect stock stories in a file. You can recycle anecdotes you've read somewhere, but tales told in the first person, in other words your own experiences, are always better.

Remember all good stories need a few basic ingredients. They must have conflict, and a resolution to that conflict. They're made even better when they have the ingredients of surprise and emotional impact. Humour, of course, is always a winner too.

Experts speak in stories. Jesus did. And most people have heard of him.

**Key question:**
Have you started a file for stock stories that illustrate your messages?

## 47. FRAME ISSUES AND CREATE URGENCY

Environmentalists have a clever communications device that is worth examining. Have you ever heard them talk about how "we only have three years left to save the world"?

Sounds startling, doesn't it? It makes a rather large, rather vague and unwieldy issue sound urgent and specific, doesn't it?

Very clever indeed.

Yet there's no possible way that statement can be validated as mathematically true. But that's not the point, is it? What they're trying to do is turn a very general idea into something that has a deadline, something specific, something urgent, so that people will pay attention to it.

Observe the difference:

"We are polluting our earth."

Result: Yawn!

"We have only three years left to save our planet, or all will be lost and our ruined carcasses will go floating through the endless vacuum of space!"

Result: Yikes!

Healthcare practitioners will often tell you that you should have your cholesterol checked. And most people realise that it's good advice. And yet they'll do absolutely nothing about it.

But transform your message to: "If you're over 25 and haven't had your cholesterol checked, your girlfriend will probably be attending your funeral within 20 years." Now you've got people's attention. Note the element of storytelling in that example too.

If your own cause, issue or message is important, but rather general, how about putting parameters to it? How about deadlines? How about employing the power of a little shock factor through consequences?

Do use accurate research and don't get caught thumb-sucking numbers. Find the numbers, find the urgency, find the meaning and turn that into a compelling message. Creating a sense of urgency is an excellent way to heighten the impact of your communications.

**Key question:**
Can you make your message urgent by setting deadlines and parameters?

## 48. CONSTANTLY MANUFACTURE MESSAGES

There's nothing quite as satisfying as having the media come to you. It's flattering, and a sure sign that you've established your expertise. But it's rare. Most of us have to put a great deal of work into becoming media notorieties and sources for answers.

So, how do you go about manufacturing a message? And how do you do it on an ongoing basis?

Here is a simple way: know your strengths and the strengths of your industry. But don't start there. Start at industry *weaknesses*. Create tension, the way advertisers do. Then provide the solution. *Your* solution.

In my case, rather than talk about great presenters, I go the route of saying: PowerPoint is undermining your chances of promotion. That's the spark that will inform my article. The rest of the article might be about solutions to that problem. Similarly, I might write an article about how presenters often duplicate material at conferences (the problem) and then speak about how they can collaborate on their presentations to make the entire day more successful (the solution). It's all about finding the pain, and providing ideas for the solution.

Let's say you're an expert wedding planner: weddings are so complex; there are a thousand things that can go wrong on your clients' special day. That means a thousand opportunities for articles, talks or thought-leadership items.

Start by identifying problems. Your solutions will then carry the underlying message: this is how I, as an expert, address that problem.

You can also get a great deal of mileage out of a single idea if you're clever about repackaging it. A speaker I once listened to at a Dallas convention of the Professional Speakers Association, Alex Mandossian, said, "You are marketing to a moving parade". It's an excellent point. You may be sick of your message, but your customer base is ever growing, ever changing, and they haven't necessarily heard it before.

And it's not just a case of continually saying the same thing through different outlets. There are clever ways of saying the same thing differently in order to get continuing publicity through the same outlets. In other words, one radio interview on a certain station, or one article in a certain magazine, need not be the end of your relationship with that outlet. Not if you learn to cleverly repackage your ideas.

Think about the bodybuilding magazines that repackage the same ideas, over and over, using different frameworks to keep them fresh.

Don't get hung up on the problem that you only have three or four article ideas. If you can think laterally enough, you can reorganise them, restate them, focus on specific parts of them, apply them to different scenarios, and keep producing almost endlessly.

Frameworks are your answer.

**Key question:**
Do you understand what essential pain you resolve?

## 49. GET MUCH, MUCH MORE MILEAGE OUT OF AN IDEA

We've already considered using frameworks to repackage ideas. Now let's maximise your publicity even further.

Do you have a system for rotating articles?

Let's say you've decided to write an article for a magazine. You have a nifty idea, too, and the editor accepts it and commits to publishing your piece. Most people would simply achieve one instance of publicity from their idea by submitting this single article to a single publication. You can do better. Rather than write ten separate articles in order to achieve ten instances of publicity, make each idea work harder for you, and achieve up to ten instances of publicity *per idea*. PR agencies understand this little trick and it's actually a simple one.

Here's how …

Subtly revise your article a number of times, particularly the opening and title, so that it's slightly different in each case, and send it to multiple publications.

Here's another way: if you're writing about one big idea, break it down into multiple parts and send it out periodically. Instead of writing one article about five ways to improve your DIY skills, write five separate, shorter articles and send them out week by week.

And here's another way still: stagger the messages you send.

Let's say you've spent the last year writing a column for your local newspaper. Now you'd like to approach a business magazine to write for them too. You don't have to start writing new articles. You already have a year's worth! You can simply submit the article that appeared a year ago in the local paper. The article will no longer clash with the one in the newspaper because they're not appearing at the same time.

Can you see how you can just keep on using this system? Another year (or less) goes by and you can start submitting the same articles to a second business magazine. You simply stagger the submissions, so each publication is running something different to the other publications at that point in time. By using this rotation principle, you could end up writing just one article per week, indefinitely, and still providing content to ten or more publications, and each one would be running unique material.

Here's another thought: the channels themselves are almost unlimited. Don't forget that the publications you see on news stands are by no means the only ones available to you. There are online ezines that work exactly like newspapers, requiring new articles daily. Some of them are highly industry specific, which can work to your advantage. Also, increasingly, corporate companies are publishing their own, very high quality inhouse magazines. Make contact with those editors. Submit your work to them. Let them know there's more available should they want it. You may even be asked to contribute a regular column, which is great for continuous profile building. Be proactive and propose a regular column.

And you're not limited to your own country, either. Next time you find yourself on an international flight or in a hotel abroad, pick up the free magazines and observe what they publish. Could you contribute? If so, email or call the editor. This is one of the wonders of the email age: you can now write for any country on earth.

Naturally, there is also great value to you in getting your work published abroad. It's somehow more exotic and "important" to be published in a foreign country: "Joanna writes articles that are published all over the world!"

Hurrah for Joanna. All it means is that Joanna knows how to use her email cleverly. But it does *sound* impressive!

**DON'T FORGET**

Organise an articles page on your website. Every time you write and submit a new article, upload it to your site. Then announce it on your various social media, and include a link. Even if you're only signed up to two social media websites, your announcements, in addition to the update on your website, will constitute another three instances of publicity.

Also, ensure that your articles are truly compelling. When they are, people pass them on. There are few things more valuable than your idea going viral.

**Key question:**
Do you have a system for maximising the effectiveness of your articles?

# 50. EXPERTS ALWAYS LEAVE A TRAIL OF BREADCRUMBS

If you go up to the hillside and they follow, you are a guru. If you go up to the hillside and they do not follow, you are merely a lost hillbilly.

You've seen over and over in the course of this book that an expert is a public construct. Experts cannot exist without the perception of a public that believes they are experts.

It follows, then, that if they can't find you, they can't use or recommend you. You cannot generate the phrase "You know who you should talk to?" if you can't be found.

I believe that there are three levels of breadcrumbs:

**LEVEL ONE**

A Level One breadcrumb is very simple. It's a means of reaching you. A business card is a Level One breadcrumb, and if you leave them behind, people can follow your trail and find you.

**LEVEL TWO**

Level Two breadcrumbs are the offer to connect and continue with a relationship. Your Facebook, Twitter or LinkedIn details are all Level Two breadcrumbs.

**LEVEL THREE**

A Level Three breadcrumb is the most desirable breadcrumb of all. It is *the offer of more*! When people see you speak, hear you being interviewed or read your articles, is there a way in which you could give them more? The offer of more free articles on your site, or a free download, which would be of benefit to them?

If you can incentivise them to follow you, you are starting to build tribes.

**Key question:**
How are you providing ways for them to find and follow you?

# PRACTICAL MECHANICS

There we are – 50 positive ideas on how to become the expert in your industry. Their potential for elevating your status is dramatic if you have the will and the discipline to act upon them. Naturally you won't use every one, and some will bring in much more dramatic results than others, but if the bulk of them informs your behaviour, they will bring you results.

Now let's consider some "Do Not's". Certain behaviours disqualify you as an industry expert, creating very poor perceptions. An expert is the construct of public perception. Ruin the perception and you are left with no more than an individual possessed of technical skills, and I've been at pains to explain that skills alone are not enough to create an expert.

**DISQUALIFYING BEHAVIOUR: "I WAS ALMOST AN EXPERT."**

Here are six kinds of disqualifying behaviour for the almost-expert:

**1. Desperation**

I think you can get away with being publically drunk with far less detriment than you can by being publically desperate. (This, however, is not a recommendation for the former.)

Desperation is the polar opposite of expert behaviour. Experts are sure of themselves, calmly confident in what they can deliver and they charge accordingly. They do not lower prices because they are not desperate for scraps. They will turn away work rather than concede that they are worth less. They negotiate from a place of strength always. Their underlying energy, though polite, is driven by the idea "*You* need *me.*"

Moreover, because they are not desperate, they engender trust. When a shifty salesperson with a sly smile promises you the moon, grinning as though he might burst, and then can't deliver it, the trust in the relationship will be short-lived. But the expert who tells you that your requirements are actually outside of his field of experience, and sends you to someone else, has massive credibility. He is not so desperate for the work that he will entertain a misfit.

### 2. The circus car arrival

"Pleasure to meet you. I'm thrilled to be here discussing this important deal. I also brought my wife, three kids and socially awkward Uncle Ernie, who we've been minding since his accident. You don't mind if they just sit in your waiting lounge while we meet, do you? They won't break much."

Image does matter, and your expertise needs to be presented with the appropriate level of decorum. Don't whine about your family issues, financial troubles or health problems in front of a client. They don't care, and it's unprofessional. You're there to discuss meeting and fulfilling their needs like a top-class practitioner.

### 3. Stealing the sugar

"Hey, look! Free stuff!"

This one is also born of desperation. It's the person who takes Tupperware to a lunch event so that they can scoop up the leftovers for later. It's taking the free sugar because you can. This behaviour is noticed, it smacks of the low-level operator and it's a silly reason to miss out on the big deals. Don't score a packet of sugar at the expense of a R100 000 contract.

### 4. The spelling mistake

The written part of your work, right down to small things like invoicing, may seem incidental to you. But people *do* notice spelling errors, they *do* comment upon them, and these comments *do* factor into their overall impressions of you. And for heavens' sake, take special care when writing the name of your client. Misspelling their name is a level of carelessness that is unforgivable. How can we be perceived as experts if we can't even get the basics right?

## 5. Neglecting the ribbon

Packaging matters. Half the excitement and, indeed, a portion of the *value* of receiving an expensive gift item, such as a pen or jewellery, is in the packaging. And high-paying clients expect it. You don't buy a diamond brooch only to have it dropped into your palm. It usually sits on a bed of velvet, in a small box, which goes into a large box, which is wrapped and placed into a gift bag that is drawn shut with a drawstring ... and a ribbon ... and some singing cherubs.

Don't neglect the ribbon in your work. Presentation matters greatly. Often, the difference between an average industry performer and an expert is not in different work quality, but different quality of presentation. Knowing this, you can raise your perceived value by raising the quality of its presentation. Make the event special for your customer. Add the ribbon.

## 6. Assuming a shared prejudice

I will never forget the "specialists" who arrived to fix my motorised gate at home, and the fat man who regaled me with his store of aggressively racist jokes. I do not share his outlook on humanity, and not only will I never use his services again, but I will actively discourage others from doing so. Why did he assume that I was a fellow racist? Who knows? The only answer I can think of is: he has no concept of professional behaviour.

# BONUS SECTION: 15 WAYS TO WIN CONTESTS

Many performance-based industries have annual contests to determine who is top of the pops. Whether you are a chef or a model, an idol or a singer, a chess master or a graphic designer, there will generally be some kind of association contest that you can enter to prove your expertise and gain extraordinary prominence.

If this is a path you would like to pursue, here are fifteen suggestions for how best to go about competing effectively. Many of these principles are as applicable to winning bids and new business as they are to winning contests:

**1. Pitch up on the day**

Try. You can't win if you don't enter. And occasionally, when contests are underattended, it can be surprising who does win, simply because that person pitched up and gave it a shot. Sometimes the competition is steep and sometimes it isn't. But if you don't arrive and throw your name into the hat on the day, you have a 100% chance of failure. Thou shalt pitch up and try.

**2. Never underestimate the competition**

Don't indulge in an "it'll do" approach. Assume your competitors will be fanatical about winning, that they will have spent months preparing, and that they are equally as talented as you. Yes, equally. Assume that your task is to outdo *yourself* on a good day. You don't want a scenario in which there is a close call between you and the second-place winner. Go about competing in such a way that the only real competition is for second and third place because you are clearly way ahead of the rest. Thy competition sleepeth not!

### 3. Learn the actual criteria

Don't assume you know what it takes to win. Find out what the judges are *actually* looking for. Generally, the judging guidelines for any contest will be made public before the contest takes place. If not, the contest is a farce, for how can competitors be expected to meet undisclosed criteria? Once you know the criteria, make sure you meet all of them, leaving nothing to chance. In the unusual event that the criteria are not available, which is often the case for tender bids, brainstorm a list of the logical probabilities. Knowledge is thy greatest power.

### 4. Bring more than the criteria

At high levels of contest in which most of your competitors are very competent, you can safely assume that just about everyone *will* meet the basic criteria. This suggests that it will take *more* than simply meeting the criteria to beat them. You have to bring something more, something extra, something magical, something memorable. Something above and beyond. What can you do to set yourself apart? Thou shalt choose to shine!

### 5. Outwork the competition

The laziness of others is your competitive advantage. Start preparing earlier. Put in longer hours. Be more organised. Practise much, much more. At high levels of competition, it is usually preparation, rather than talent, that separates first from second place. 2001 Public Speaking World Champion, Darren LaCroix, states that the three most important ways to become a championship-winning speaker are: stage time, stage time and stage time. Performance specialists advocate that 10 000 hours of deliberate practice at your craft will make you a master practitioner. Put in the stage time and it shall pay thee massive dividends.

## 6. Play to your strengths

If there is anything that naturally sets you apart, play it up to the best of your ability. Design your competitive approach in such a way that it highlights and showcases your strengths. As a speaker, I'm often told that my voice is my greatest asset, and so I make sure that my speech scripts give me plenty of opportunity for vocal range. Thou shalt show off thy glories.

## 7. Minimise your weaknesses

If there's anything you struggle with, find ways to minimise how visible those weaknesses are. Design your competitive approach to play them down. If you are the bodybuilder with the smallest calf muscles, don't stand next to the one with the biggest. If you can avoid foregrounding a weak point, do so. Thou shalt soften thy infirmities.

## 8. Use mentors

You can evaluate your own performance by watching yourself in a mirror, or viewing a video recording of your rehearsals. But you will only see so much. You need fresh eyes, a fresh mind. You need a mentor or mentors. Ultimately, it's your call as to what advice you take to heart and what you discard, but listen to their input and be open to their suggestions. Thy teacher shall help thee grow.

## 9. Research the history

The most valuable thing I ever did for my own competitive speaking was to watch videos of the past World Championship contests. Before watching them, I was clueless. After watching them, I was left in a state of disbelief at how unprepared I was and how developed the winning speeches were. This was my single greatest learning curve. It's logical: you can't win the Mr Olympia contest without knowing what the reigning champion is doing. Also, watch television's *Idols* to see how many competitors make the same mistakes that have been made – and pointed out – a thousand times before. That doesn't have to be you. Learn the history of your contest. Study the winners, and learn where the traps are. Find out what it *really* takes. Thou shalt study the annals.

## 10. Be the one people want to win

Poor sportsmanship and sleazy politicking are counterproductive. Be an honest competitor and a decent human being. Wish others well and compete sincerely. In that way, when the judges, who are only human too, are faced with a tight decision, they will want you to win. The crowd will do the same and show you greater support. Thy good name is thy greatest ally.

## 11. Don't indulge in self-disqualifying behaviour

Supplying silly reasons why you shouldn't win. Don't do it. If you're supposed to wear a certain uniform, do so. If a certain move would lose points for you, avoid it. If there are time limits, stick to them. Don't supply the judges with any excuse, however trivial, to drop you by the wayside. If it's a close call for first place, don't be the competitor who supplies the authorities with a reason to give it to the other person. Thou shalt not senselessly disqualify thyself.

## 12. Check out the venue

Technicalities can trip you up. Find out about the venue, and how it will be organised, in advance. You may be planning something that requires a certain amount of space, and be unpleasantly surprised by a restricted performance or display area on the day. Know thy venue, and how it shall affect thee.

## 13. On the day don't be the bride who fainted

On their big wedding day, it is not uncommon for brides to become so swept up in the excitement that they don't have breakfast, skip lunch and drink nothing but champagne ... then become one more statistic to faint at the altar. Make sure you plan the simple but necessary logistics surrounding the day itself, so that your mental and physical performance is not impeded by small oversights. Thou need not faint at the altar.

**14. Develop a "big game" temperament**

Contests rely heavily on psychology. If you are intimidated by your competitors, you will probably underperform and lose. Curiously, the abilities of your competitors will always seem greatly enhanced to you on the day. That's because you have become familiar with your own performance and level of skill. But to others, your performance and skill levels are equally fresh and equally daunting. Don't worry about how good the competition appears. Relax. Focus on your own sphere of control, and enjoy what *you* do.

**15. Don't ever, ever cheat**

Reputations do not recover from cheating. Ask Lance.

# SOME FINAL THOUGHTS

**THE ETHOS OF THE WORLD CHAMPION**

In Toastmasters circles, the winner of each year's World Championships for Public Speaking becomes a sort of instant celebrity. And each World Champion contributes to the total wisdom of the organisation's membership by speaking at conferences on their experiences, the lessons they learnt along the way to the championships and the strategies they employed to win the contest. Some also produce books, and audio and video programmes. These producers also tend to be the ones whose legacies last the longest.

One World Champion, Craig Valentine, once made an interesting remark, not about his journey *to* the contest, but about his continued journey *afterwards*. He said that the first thing he did, the very next day after winning the Public Speaking World Championships, was to go out and buy a book on public speaking!

Remarkable. And admirable.

This man is indisputably an authority in his field. He is a *World Champion*, an absolute public title.

And yet, he maintains an attitude of humility and a desire for learning. He is still hungry for growth. He remains humble and open to knowledge. One might argue that this is *why* he won the World Championships in the first place.

This quality will also give him longevity in the field. When others have grown stale and outdated, he will still be strong, vibrant and relevant. This willingness to remain a perpetual student, even at expert levels, will separate the truly great from the merely good. It is the distinction between a flash-in-the-pan moment of excellence and true, sustained legend. Moreover, it will keep the truly great right at the top of their game as they constantly revise and renew their already considerable knowledge base.

**IN THE REAL WORLD**

This life approach – maintaining the attitude of a perpetual student – is not just theoretical either. There is a practical application for such an ethos.

Many experts find themselves carrying out the same basic procedure many times over. For instance, as a financial planning expert, you might find yourself giving the same presentation repeatedly all around the country.

It's good enough. You've become noted on the strength of it. And it's easy simply to keep repeating a winning formula.

But if you have the ethos of the ever-growing expert, you will continually look for ways to improve upon it. You might workshop certain segments. You might read books on how to add humour or vibrancy to your presentations, and apply the techniques you have learnt. You might even survey audiences, and elicit feedback on their likes and dislikes, and what they might want more of.

Not only does this keep your skills sharply honed, but it also staves off boredom.

If you plan to do this, do it in an intelligent way. Don't just ask for feedback on your performance. Set criteria. Ask them to evaluate a few specified things in isolated detail. In the case of a presentation, you might ask for feedback on specific stories, or your use of voice, or your visuals. Don't just ask them to rate your speech out of ten because this doesn't provide you with any useful growth information.

**FAILURES AS FUEL: WHY SETBACKS CAN BE YOUR GREATEST BOOSTERS**

Failure is an interesting divider of people. Some of us experience failure and we grow bitter, contract spiritually and become less. Some of us use it to grow. To propel ourselves and become more.

I believe that your reaction to failure is a choice.

A few years back, I had reached a period of some complacency in my own career. Things were going well, and so I had started coasting. I was no longer writing books or articles, no longer putting very much effort into my marketing. Things were rolling along just fine so I became lax.

Then the recession of 2009 hit and everything changed. Long-term contracts that had been the mainstay of my earnings suddenly dried up. With speakers and trainers perceived as an expensive luxury, large corporations battened down the hatches and clung to their training and event budgets. Life suddenly became very interesting.

This rude awakening thrust me into emergency mode, and changed my scenario from that of relative prosperity to a sudden case of sink-or-swim.

I went into hyper drive. I had to re-employ all of the techniques I had used to build my career in the first place. I got in touch with old clients. I made new contacts with agents and editors. I started writing again for publications that I sought out on the racks of bookstores and online. I did everything I could to reassert my position as a valuable expert in addition to my *relevance* to my market.

It was a frightening time for me, and there were many months in which I seriously wondered whether I was going to survive or not. "Not" became a harrowing possibility. It's almost amusing to look at your life in purely academic terms and think, "Hmm, it is entirely possible that I might not actually make it. Fascinating!" It is equally enthralling to look at your car and wonder when angry men will be arriving to take it away.

Nevertheless, with work, sweat, toil, prayers, tears, and an almost supernatural level of strategy and effort, I pulled through. I accumulated a huge amount of financial debt in the process. I lost sleep. But I survived.

Ultimately, as a result of this period of what James A. Michener would term "an indecent display of industry", my business actually became stronger than ever.

On the far side of this awful period of great stress and distress, my wife made the comment, "This might just have been the best thing that ever happened to you."

No, she doesn't have a sadistic sense of humour (okay, she does, but in this case, she was actually being sincere). She made this observation because I had been running on nothing but momentum.

Remember one of our earliest expert positioning techniques? Don't just choose to be good; make the decision to be the very best? "Good enough" being the enemy of greatness, in this period of failure and need, of fright and dissatisfaction, may just have been the most important period of growth in my entire career. It was a wake-up call of note, and it showed me what I could actually do if my survival depended upon it. She was right. It was the best thing for me.

Failure is a kind of fuel. Problems are a catalyst for growth.

Ease is death. Where there is no challenge, there will be no advancement.

Of course, when you find yourself in survival mode, it's not easy to be quite so philosophical and acknowledge with joyful plaintiveness, "Happy day! This is good for me". But the reality is that trying times truly are an opportunity to grow.

I even see this principle at work in my exercise regimen. If I have a day when I'm able to lift less weight than usual, it plays on my mind until I become so frustrated that I often go out and not only *match* my old weight-lifting records but, in many cases, exceed them.

This is yet another example of how small-scale perceived failures can be used to spur on accomplishment. However, the key difference between a downhill slope and a period of advancement and growth is always *choice.* When faced with failures, on any scale, you must *choose* to use the incident to inspire more from yourself. If you don't make the choice to use failures constructively, then they become merely the beginning of a downhill slope.

Don't choose to see them as failures. Chose to see them as fuel. They really can be your friends. Ride them with sufficient intensity, and on the far side, you just might discover that you have become noteworthy in your industry.

**MY WISH FOR YOU**

I'm grateful that you have invested time in reading my book on expert positioning. I hope that you have read it simply because you wish to be more, and not because you are in a desperate financial situation. But either way, these ideas can help you. They can place you on the mountainside with followers at your feet. They can improve your status, your business and your income. They can increase your joy in what you do.

It is noteworthy that occupying a place on the hillside makes you a leader. I hope that you will use your elevated position to benefit others, and lift them up in turn. I hope that you will use your skills, talents and opportunities to bless.

Expert positioning is not a selfish pursuit. Would it not be an insult to your creator *not* to become the highest, most developed, most incredible version of yourself that you possibly can?

The greatest experts are the greatest teachers and mentors. And even when they are purely performers, they are capable of spreading immense joy through what they do. As was the case with Michael Jackson, one of the greatest creators, producers and performers of the previous century, and a man still lauded as a once-in-a-lifetime legend.

Perhaps it is apt, then, that having referenced Michael in our early expert positioning techniques, we quote him now at the end:

Consciousness expresses itself through creation. This world we live in is the dance of the creator. Dancers come and go in the twinkling of an eye but the dance lives on. On many an occasion when I am dancing, I have felt touched by something sacred. In those moments, I felt my spirit soar and become one with everything that exists.

I become the stars and the moon. I become the lover and the beloved. I become the victor and the vanquished. I become the master and the slave. I become the singer and the song. I become the knower and the known. I keep on dancing then it is the eternal dance or creation. The creator and creation merge into one wholeness of joy. I keep on dancing ... and dancing ... and dancing. Until there is only ... the dance. – Michael Jackson, *Dangerous*

Dancing is life. – Stephen King, *11/22/63*

# YOUR QUICK CHEAT SHEETS

**REVISITING THE KEY QUESTIONS**

- Have you made the decision to be at the top of your game?
- What do you want to stand for?
- Are you hungrier than your peers and competitors?
- Are you constantly looking for information on how to become more?
- Do you know where to source sufficient reading materials on your topic to fuel an hour of reading each day?
- Are you prostituting yourself by doing a little bit of everything, or have you found your area of focus?
- When people think about your industry, why should they think about you?
- What is your plan to go from a name on a piece of paper, to a living person in the forefront of important players' minds?
- Which people or associations can boost your credibility?
- Is your look distinctive and memorable?
- Does your public persona match the real you?
- Do you know who you are and how you are ranked in relation to the key players?
- Can you sum up *what you are* in a short phrase?
- What is the simplest, most to-the-point title for what you do?
- What have you overcome in order to be what you are?
- How much greater could you be if you *really* tried?
- What sort of handout would your target market truly appreciate?
- What more could you do to generate references and referrals?
- What could you set up this week that would translate directly into results?

- Do you know what fees the top players currently command?
- Have you developed an introduction for others to use?
- What sort of book, relating to your industry, would *you* buy and read?
- How many hours will pass, from right now, until you submit your first article?
- Whose online updates do you personally follow, because they are genuinely interesting?
- How many third parties are on your list to approach regarding endorsement, and how do you plan to impress them?
- Which organisations have similar goals to yours and might consider a partnership?
- What is your unique signature?
- When it comes to your unique framework philosophy, is there a way of organising your mountain of dots 'n dashes into something that people can instantly "get"?
- What visual or graphic opportunities could you exploit to create greater presence and visibility?
- If you were a journalist, what sort of publicity event would hook your interest?
- Which shows could you appear on to discuss issues, and what additional issues could you cover for greater mileage?
- How many of your marketing and communication elements currently have different branding tones?
- What is your deeper agenda during important expert-positioning scenarios?
- If you're honest with yourself, when last were you *not* true to your word?
- Are you in the habit of returning all communications, quickly?
- What can you do to make your enablers look good in the eyes of their clients?
- Does negative media put you into a state of emotional lockdown, or do you seek out the opportunity in the storm?
- Are you charging at the mid-to-upper levels of your industry?
- Do you sell from a place of desperation?
- Could your guarantee be in some way more impressive than your competitors'?
- Are the key marketing phrases in your terminology toolbox catchy and memorable?
- What issue are you strongly opposed to in your industry that can be turned into a rallying cry?

- What free education can you give away, with the underlying message that you are the best in the business?
- Are you apologising for your statements with passive tense language?
- Based on issues in your industry, what catchphrases could you develop that sum up a concept quickly?
- Are you like the empty husk that never developed a metaphor?
- Have you started a file for stock stories that illustrate your messages?
- Can you make your message urgent by setting deadlines and parameters?
- Do you understand what essential pain you resolve?
- How are you providing ways for them to find and follow you?

## 10 ROOKIE ERRORS TO AVOID

### 1. Being a weasel

The kind of person who says, "That's what I said" when it really wasn't. Don't be a slippery operator; you will get caught.

### 2. Falling apart when the world around you falls apart

Things *will* go wrong. Keep your head. Do the best you can with what you have. People are watching you so don't lose the plot. It is what it is. Move on.

### 3. Coming on too strong

I'll never forget the agent who told me about a certain speaker she refuses to work with simply because he came on too strong. "'You MUST use me' is not the sort of language I want to hear," she said.

### 4. Getting the PA to call key people who you should call yourself

You think it looks impressive. The key person thinks you're not showing respect. "Couldn't even be bothered to pick up the phone and talk to me himself!"

### 5. Short-changing an agent

Always charge the same exit price as your agency, even though they're charging a commission. Don't incentivise your agent's customers to cut them out of the loop and seek you out at cheaper prices. Sure, it might mean a little extra cash now, but you will damage your relationship with your agent in the long run. Also, when you get repeat business, which was originally booked by your agent, give them their commission again. It's only ethical and it's a good relationship move.

### 6. Getting drunk at public events

You'd be surprised. One agent commented to me that a sports star she liked to recommend as a speaker became intoxicated at not one, but two events. Now, every time an event comes up for which he is well suited, she is faced with a dilemma. Don't indulge in self-disqualifying behaviour.

### 7. Crude sexual advances on key people

Flirtation has its place. But there are few things tackier than a crude sexual advance on a key player, particularly if you, or the key player, happens to be married. Be discerning about what you can and cannot get away with.

### 8. Winging it

Never underperform during a public appearance. These are your forums, and should be taken very seriously. Consistent excellence adds up to a favourable reputation. Take every event seriously, even the "little" ones.

### 9. Slating the competition

Good sportsmanship and a disciplined tongue are hallmarks of a competitor who is secure in his or her own ability. Slating the competition makes you look bitter, lesser and, in certain cases, a bit pathetic.

**10. Resting on your laurels**

Unless they are constantly innovating, constantly producing and constantly publicising, experts are quickly forgotten.

# REFERENCES

Article Titles on p.97 from Muscle & Fitness Magazine. (n.d.).

BMW South Africa (Producer). (2007). *Test Pilot* [Television Advertisment]. Gauteng: Broadcast Nationally.

Calloway, J. (2009). *Becoming a Category of One: How Extraordinary Companies Transcend Commodity and Defy Comparison (2nd ed.)*. New Jersey: John Wiley & Sons.

CBS News (2011). *Dr. Phil thanks Oprah for his start in TV*. Retrieved 2014, from CBSNews.com: http://www.cbsnews.com/news/dr-phil-thanks-oprah-for-his-start-in-tv/

*Clarkonisms*. (2008-2011). Retrieved from Clarkonisms: http://www.clarksonisms.com/

Cohen, J. (2011, June 17). *Why don't people achieve their goals?* Retrieved 2014, from Justinpresents: http://www.justinpresents.com/jchome/why-dont-people-achieve-their-goals/

Colvin, G. (2008). *Talent is Overrated: What Really Separates World-Class Performers from Everybody Else*. New York: Portfolio Penguin.

David Galland. (2014). *Casey Gems—David Galland on the True Secret of Success*. Retrieved from Casey Research: http://www.caseyresearch.com/articles/casey-gemsdavid-galland-on-the-true-secret-of-success

Davies, A. (2013). *Analysts Say Bugatti Loses $6.24 Million For Every Veyron Supercar It Sells*. Retrieved 2014, from Business Insider: http://www.businessinsider.com/bugatti-may-lose-6-million-per-veyron-2013-10

Frears, S. (Director). (2007). *The Queen* [Motion Picture].

Gage, R. (2012). *Educational Session*. PSA Winter Conference. Dallas, Texas.

*George Bernard Shaw Quotes*. (2014, January 29). Retrieved from Wikiquote: http://en.wikiquote.org/wiki/George_Bernard_Shaw

Gladwell, M. (2000). *The Tipping Point: How Little Things Can Make a Big Difference*. New York: Back Bay Books.

Gladwell, M. (2008). *Outliers: The Story of Success*. New York: Little, Brown and Company.

Jackson, M. (1991). *Dangerous* [CD Booklet]. New York: Epic Records.

*Jon Bon Jovi Quotes*. (2014). Retrieved from Celebrity Quotes: http://www.celebritiesquotes.com/Jon-Bon-Jovi-Quotes.php

Key, J. (2001). *No Doubt!* 2001 Toastmasters Public Speaking World Championships. Anaheim, California.

King, S. ( 2011). *11/22/63*. New York: Scribner.

King, S. (2000). *On Writing: A Memoir of the Craft*. London: Hodder and Stoughton.

Mandossian, A. (2012). *Educational Session*. PSA Winter Conference. Dallas, Texas.

McKeith, G. (Presenter). (2008). Ban Big Bums. In *Supersize vs Superskinny* [Television Broadcast]. UK: Channel 4.

Michener, J. A. (1990). *The Eagle and the Raven*. Buffalo Gap: State House Press.

National Speakers Association. (2011 and 2012). *Voices of Experience*. Retrieved from iTunes: https://itunes.apple.com/us/podcast/the-nsa-podcast-network/id310026074?mt=2

Ortega, K. (Director). (2010). *This is It!* [Motion Picture].

*Paul Naidoo Information*. (2014). Retrieved from Famous Faces Management: http://www.famousfaces.co.za/Artist.aspx/Id/593/Active/Speaker/Speaker_Motivational/Speaker_Sales_and_Marketing/hide

Portas, M. (Presenter). (2008). Blinkz. In *Mary Queen of Shops* [Television Broadcast]. UK: BBC One.

*Professional Summarizer*. (2012). Retrieved from DaleIrvin.com: http://www.daleirvin.com/summarizer.htm

Robinson, P. A. (Director). (1989). *Field of Dreams* [Motion Picture].

Walter, B. (2012). *Educational Session*. PSA Winter Conference. Dallas, Texas.

Weiss, A. (2011). *Million Dollar Speaking: The Professional's Guide to Building Your Platform*. New York: McGraw-Hill.

*Own Your Industry* is a guide to the practical things you can do to position yourself as the guru, the thought leader, the "go-to-name" in your industry. Because when you are known as the best, *they* will come to you.

Perceptions, managed and accumulated over time, are the stuff experts are made of.

Being perceived as an amateur is undesirable and unprofitable. But if you aspire to become widely revered as the thought leader in your sphere, you will need to learn how to frame issues in the media, how to communicate complex ideas through particular structures and the ways in which your fees may peg you as a beginner or a veteran.

Douglas Kruger, five-times winner of the Southern African Public Speaking Championships and full-time professional speaker, author and trainer, is recognised as the pre-eminent public speaking expert in South Africa. In this book, he explains how to develop a title, become a face and a voice in the minds of key industry players and use simple positioning techniques to cut through the marketing clutter of your competitors.

This book is ideal for anyone building a business or a personal brand. It's particularly useful for entrepreneurs who want a better understanding of what it takes to be perceived as the best.

Create tribes. Develop reputation. Become the answer to the question, "You know who you should talk to?"

Don't settle for the scraps beneath the table. Being an amateur is undesirable and unprofitable. Become an expert. And have the media, the clientele and the key players come to *you*. Learn how in Douglas Kruger's *Own Your Industry*.

Douglas Kruger is a professional speaker and trainer, and author of the *50 Ways* series of books. He is South Africa's only five-times winner of the Southern African Championships for Public Speaking. Douglas is based in Johannesburg, but speaks and trains all over the world. See him at www.douglaskruger.co.za. Read his articles on www.douglaskruger.com.

Follow him on LinkedIn or Twitter: @douglaskruger.